Treasures

Grade 5

Grammar

AND

Writing

Handbook

 Macmillan/McGraw-Hill

A

The *McGraw·Hill* Companies

**Macmillan
McGraw-Hill**

Published by Macmillan/McGraw-Hill, of McGraw-Hill Education, a division of The McGraw-Hill Companies, Inc.,
Two Penn Plaza, New York, New York 10121.

Printed in the United States of America

1 2 3 4 5 6 7 8 9 079 11 10 09 08 07

Writing

Contents

Contents

Writing

Writing

Grammar

Contents

Build Skills

Troubleshooter

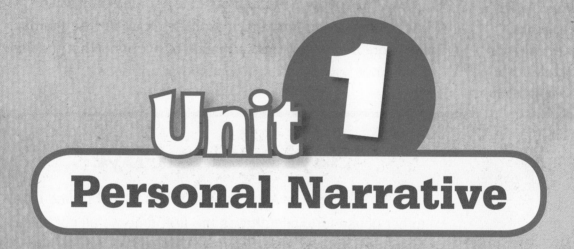

Unit 1
Personal Narrative

Personal Narrative

Can you think of an interesting story to tell someone about yourself? A story that tells about a personal experience is called a personal narrative. A personal narrative brings to life a memorable event. It tells what happened and how the writer felt about the experience.

Learning from Writers

Read the following examples of a personal narrative. What stories do the writers share? Think about the words the writers use to tell the sequence of events. What did they say to show how they felt about the experience?

THINK AND WRITE

Purpose
Why do people like to write personal narratives? Why do other people like to read them? Jot down your thoughts in your journal.

Saying Good-Bye

The night before Aunt Waka left, Mrs. Sugar invited us all to her house for dinner. It was the first time we all got invited together, and Mrs. Sugar used her best china and her plated silverware and baked a big ham.

She gave Aunt Waka a beaded coin purse and several hugs and said she might even go to Japan someday to visit her.

And Aunt Waka said, "I'll be waiting for you," just the way she said she'd wait for me.

The next morning, Mama, Papa, Joji, and I took Aunt Waka to San Francisco to the same pier where we'd gone to meet her. Another big ship was berthed there, waiting to take her back to Japan.

—Yoshiko Uchida, from *A Jar of Dreams*

Starting the Week

I'm a pretty easygoing sort of person, and it takes a lot to get me upset. When I woke up yesterday, I had no idea of what was in store. There was a huge amount of math homework due, but I had done the work in no time. I was looking forward to the play rehearsal, too.

At school, the math teacher collected our homework. No wonder it had seemed so easy—I had done the wrong pages! The rest of the morning was fine, except I nearly sprained my jaw trying to eat the snack I had packed in my backpack. It turned out to be a rubber cookie that Wendy had slipped in.

At last it was time for our play rehearsal. "Break a leg," said Denise. The doctor laughed so hard when I told him the story that I almost kicked him with the plaster cast he had just put on my left foot.

—Markus Baker

PRACTICE AND APPLY

Thinking Like a Reader

1. In the correct order, name the sequence of events from "Saying Good-Bye."

2. Summarize "Starting the Week" by telling its beginning, middle, and end.

Thinking Like a Writer

3. What time-order words did the author use to tell you the order of events in "Saying Good-Bye"?

4. How did the author of "Starting the Week" use paragraphs to organize his personal narrative?

5. **Reading Across Texts** Compare the personal experiences of the two writers. Write about how their feelings might have been alike or different.

Personal Narrative

GUIDELINES

A personal narrative is a form of writing that tells what happened to you, including what you did and how you felt about the experience. A good personal narrative:

▶ tells a story from **personal experience**.

▶ expresses the writer's feelings by using the **first-person point of view**.

▶ has an interesting **beginning, middle**, and **end**.

▶ shares events in a **sequence** that makes sense.

▶ uses **time-order words** to connect ideas and show the sequence of events.

▶ A Personal Experience

Reread "Saying Good-Bye" by Yoshiko Uchida on page 8. Who is the narrative about? How do you think the writer felt?

> And Aunt Waka said, "I'll be waiting for you," just the way she said she'd wait for me.

The word *me* refers to the author, who is also the narrator. *Aunt Waka* refers to the author's aunt. These clues tell you that the narrative is about these two people.

▶ First-Person Point of View

Yoshiko Uchida's personal narrative uses this sentence to tell what happened during a family dinner. How do you know that the account is based on the author's personal experience? From whose point of view is the story being told?

> It was the first time we all got invited together, and Mrs. Sugar used her best china and her plated silverware and baked a big ham.

The word *we* indicates that the author was part of the action and is describing her personal observations.

► An Interesting Beginning, Middle, and End

A strong narrative needs to include an interesting beginning, middle, and end. Reread the following sentence from the final paragraph.

> Another big ship was berthed there, waiting to take her back to Japan.

What did you learn about the end of the visit?

► Sequence of Events

Yoshiko Uchida tells the events of her aunt's visit in a logical order. Notice that the first sentence tells the reader when the events in the paragraph begin.

> The night before Aunt Waka left, Mrs. Sugar invited us all to her house for dinner.

What phrase tells you when the event took place?

► Time-Order Words

To help your readers understand your experience from beginning to end, you can use time-order words and phrases. Some examples of time-order words are *first, before,* and *next*.

> The next morning, Mama, Papa, Joji, and I took Aunt Waka to San Francisco to the same pier where we'd gone to meet her.

What time-order phrase did the author use?

PRACTICE AND APPLY

Create a Features Chart

1. List the features of a good personal narrative.
2. Reread "Starting the Week" by Markus Baker on page 9.
3. Write one example of each feature of Markus's writing.
4. Write what you liked best about Markus's personal narrative.

Features	Examples

11

Prewrite

A personal narrative is a true story that describes an event or experience from your life. Writing a personal narrative allows you to share an experience with other people.

Purpose and Audience

The purpose of writing a personal narrative is to express your thoughts and feelings about an experience. It is also to interest and entertain your readers, or audience.

Before writing, you need to think about your audience. Who will be reading your personal narrative? How will you speak to your audience through your writing? How will you order your events and present your ideas?

Choose a Topic

Begin your writing by making a list of your memorable experiences. Think about which experience you would like most to share.

After choosing a topic, **explore ideas** by making a list of events or details that you remember about your experience. Also include some of your thoughts and feelings about the events. Later, you will organize these ideas.

THINK AND WRITE

Audience

How will your audience influence the topic you choose for your personal narrative? Write your ideas in your journal.

Here is how I explored my ideas.

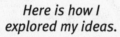

Meeting My Summer Goal

Set a goal to swim across the lake at camp

Made a plan to meet my goal

Told my family about my plan

Asked the counselors to help me train

My favorite counselor's name was Derek

Trained for weeks

The water shined

People came to cheer me on

Linda videotaped the event

Someone rowed alongside me in a boat

I ended up meeting my goal

Organize • Main Idea and Details

A personal narrative develops from one main idea. You then add supporting details to the main idea to develop your narrative. To plan your personal narrative, you can use a main idea map. Some details may not be important to include in your story. What details from his list did the writer leave out of his chart?

PREWRITE

DRAFT

REVISE

PROOFREAD

PUBLISH

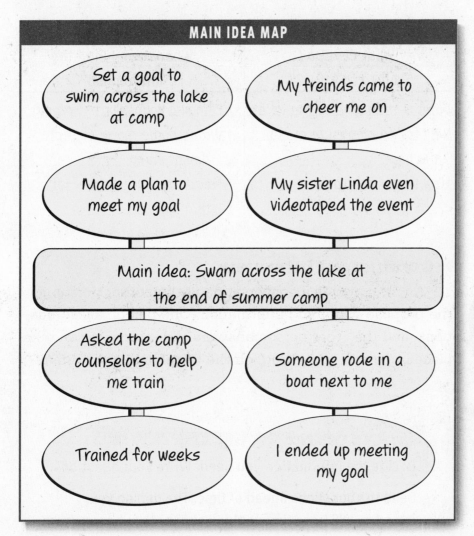

MAIN IDEA MAP

Set a goal to swim across the lake at camp

My freinds came to cheer me on

Made a plan to meet my goal

My sister Linda even videotaped the event

Main idea: Swam across the lake at the end of summer camp

Asked the camp counselors to help me train

Someone rode in a boat next to me

Trained for weeks

I ended up meeting my goal

PRACTICE AND APPLY

Plan Your Own Personal Narrative

1. Think about your purpose and audience.

2. Brainstorm a list of memorable experiences.

3. Choose a topic and explore ideas about it.

4. Use a main idea map to organize your ideas.

Checklist ✓

Prewriting

- ■ Did you think about your purpose and audience?

- ■ Did you make a list of experiences?

- ■ Did you choose a topic and explore ideas?

- ■ Did you use a chart to organize your ideas?

- ■ Did you support your main idea with important details?

- ■ Do you need to do any research?

Prewrite • Research and Inquiry

▶ Writer's Resources

You may have to do research to get more information for your personal narrative. Begin by writing a list of questions. Then decide what resources you need in order to answer each question.

What Else Do I Need to Know?	Where Can I Find the Information?
What is the name of the lake?	E-mail a counselor to find out.
Who rowed alongside me in the boat?	Watch home movie of that day at camp.
How long did I train?	Read my diary entries for that summer.

▶ Conduct an Interview

An interview is a conversation with another person for the purpose of gaining information. One person asks questions, and the other person answers. An interview can take place in person, in writing, on the telephone, or by e-mail.

STRATEGIES FOR INTERVIEWING

• Decide the information you need. Write your questions.

• Send the questions ahead of time. The person you interview will have time to think about his or her answers.

• Take clear notes and organize them right after the interview so you won't forget the information.

• Be polite and friendly. Always thank the person at the end of the interview.

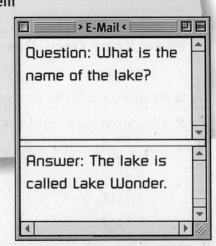

> E-Mail ‹

Question: What is the name of the lake?

Answer: The lake is called Lake Wonder.

▶ Study Personal Records

Souvenirs, photographs, journals, and home movies can be useful sources of information. Look for specific details in these sources that will help your readers "see" the event.

▶ Use Your Research

This writer learned something important in his e-mail interview. He also found information in his diary and in a video his sister made. How did he change his chart?

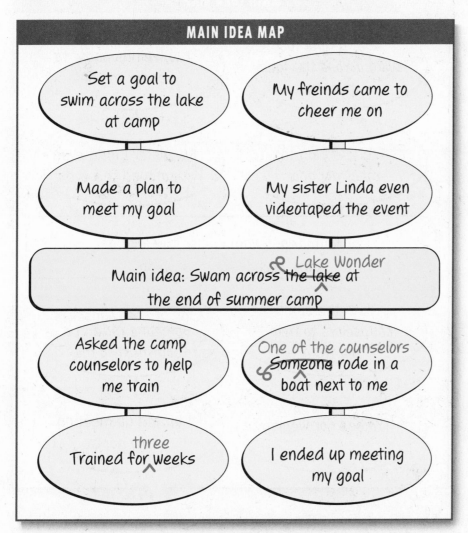

MAIN IDEA MAP

Set a goal to swim across the lake at camp

My freinds came to cheer me on

Made a plan to meet my goal

My sister Linda even videotaped the event

Main idea: Swam across the lake at ^Lake Wonder the end of summer camp

Asked the camp counselors to help me train

One of the counselors ^Someone rode in a boat next to me

Trained for ^three weeks

I ended up meeting my goal

PRACTICE AND APPLY

Review Your Plan

1. Look at your main idea map.
2. List questions you have about your topic.
3. Identify the resources you will need to find answers.
4. Add new information you gather to your chart.

Checklist ✓

Research and Inquiry

- Did you write a list of questions?
- Did you identify possible resources?
- Did you take notes on the information you found?
- Did you add the new information to your chart?

Draft

Writing PROCESS

Before you begin writing your personal narrative, review your main idea map. Think about the paragraphs you could write to support the main idea. Include details in a logical order.

Main idea for first paragraph: Why I decided to swim across the lake.

✓ Checklist

Drafting

- Does your narrative suit your purpose and audience?

- Did you include time-order words to show the sequence of events?

- Did you include your thoughts and feelings to make your writing personal?

- Did you use sensory details that will help your reader create a mental picture?

- Is your main idea clear, and do your details help your readers feel as though they were at the event?

MAIN IDEA MAP

Set a goal to swim across the lake at camp

My freinds came to cheer me on

Made a plan to meet my goal

My sister Linda even videotaped the event

Main idea: Swam across the lake at ^Lake Wonder^ the end of summer camp

Asked the camp counselors to help me train

One of the counselors ^Someone^ rode in a boat next to me

three Trained for ^weeks

I ended up meeting my goal

Main idea for second paragraph: How I trained.

Main idea for third paragraph: How I met my goal.

Look at how this writer used the ideas in her map to write a first draft. He created paragraphs by telling his story in order and by using details.

DRAFT

Last summer, I went to camp. I go to the same camp every year. Last summer was diffrent. That was the summer I decided to swim across Lake Wonder.

Main idea of first paragraph

I knew it wouldn't be easy. I made a plan to meet my goal. I asked the camp counselors to help me train. After three weeks of training in and out of the water, it was time.

Supporting details tell how the writer trained for the swimming event.

My freinds came to cheer me on as I jumped in and began to swim. My sister Linda even videotaped the event one of the counselors rowed in a boat next to me for safety. It wasn't easy, but I made it. Meeting my goal was the perfect end to the summer

Supporting details tell about the events and how the writer felt about the experience.

PRACTICE AND APPLY

Draft Your Own Personal Narrative

1. Review your prewriting chart.
2. Write about the events in the order they happened.
3. Add details that tell about the main idea.
4. Use the *I* point of view throughout to tell about the events and your feelings.

TECHNOLOGY

Find out how to adjust line spacing on your computer. Double-space your draft so you will have more room to make revisions.

Revise

Elaborate

One way to improve your writing is to elaborate. When you elaborate, you add important ideas and details that might be missing from your writing. When you revise your personal narrative, you may need to tell more about your feelings.

The writer added details to let his audience know how he felt.

> After three weeks of training in and out of the
> *I finally felt ready*
> water, ~~it was time~~.

The writer added the name of the camp to give more true information to his story.

> *Camp Wilderness*
> Last summer, I went to ~~camp~~.

Word Choice

When you are writing, it is important to choose the right words for your topic and audience.

In a personal narrative, choose words that will help you tell the events of your story in order. This will enable your reader to "see" the events in the order in which they happened.

> *First,*
> I made a plan to meet my goal. *Next,* I asked the camp
> *Then,*
> counselors to help me train. After three weeks of
> *I finally felt ready*
> training in and out of the water, ~~it was time~~.

TIME-ORDER WORDS

first

next

then

later

last

finally

now

one day

before

after

after that

as soon as

yesterday

today

tomorrow

Better Sentences

PREWRITE

DRAFT

REVISE

PROOFREAD

PUBLISH

As you continue to revise your draft, check your sentences to make sure they fit together well and flow smoothly. Read the sentences aloud. How do they sound? Have you included different types of sentences? By using a variety of sentences, such as questions, exclamations, and commands, you can make your writing more interesting to read.

Sometimes you can use an exclamation to show emotion. Notice how the writer expresses his strong feelings about having achieved his goal.

> How excited I was when I made it across the lake
> ~~It wasn't easy, but I made it~~
> ^

PRACTICE AND APPLY

Revise Your Own Personal Narrative

1. Use time-order words to show the sequence of events.

2. Use vivid and exact words to create a clear image in the reader's mind.

3. Add important details that will make your writing clearer and more accurate.

5. **Grammar** Did you use different types of sentences to make your writing more interesting?

TECHNOLOGY

Review your draft to see if the sentences follow a logical order. Do the ideas flow smoothly? If not, try moving paragraphs or sentences around by cutting and pasting text.

Revise • Peer Conferencing

Take a break from your writing. Exchange your draft with a partner, and check each other's work. Your partner may be able to give you some new ideas or suggestions on how to improve your narrative.

This beginning makes me want to read more!

This helps me to see your plan.

You should describe the water so that your readers can see it.

I think you need a third paragraph.

Last summer, I went to camp. I go to the same camp every year. Last summer was diffrent.

That was the summer I decided to swim across Lake Wonder.

I knew it wouldn't be easy. I made a plan to meet my goal. I asked the camp counselors to help me train. After three weeks of training in and out of the water, it was time. My freinds came to cheer me on as I jumped in and began to swim. My sister Linda even videotaped the event one of the counselors rowed in a boat next to me for safety. It wasn't easy, but I made it. Meeting my goal was the perfect end to the summer

Conferencing for the Reader

■ Are features of a personal narrative included in your partner's piece?
- personal experience
- first-person point of view
- interesting beginning, middle, and end
- logical sequence
- time-order words
- strong ending

■ Be sure to tell your partner what's good about the piece as well as what needs improvement.

As you revise your personal narrative, consider the comments and suggestions your conferencing partner gave you. This writer made some changes based on his partner's suggestions.

PREWRITE

DRAFT

REVISE

PROOFREAD

PUBLISH

REVISE

~~The Perfect Summer Ending~~

Camp Wilderness

Last summer, I went to ~~camp.~~ I go to the same camp every year. Last summer was diffrent.

That was the summer I decided to swim across Lake Wonder.

First,

I knew it wouldn't be easy. I made a plan to meet

Next,

my goal. I asked the camp counselors to help me

Then, shimmering blue

train. After three weeks of training in and out of the

I finally felt ready

water, ~~it was time.~~ My freinds came to cheer me on

as I jumped in and began to swim. My sister Linda

even videotaped the event one of the counselors

rowed in a boat next to me for safety. ~~It wasn't easy,~~

How excited I was when I made it across the lake

~~but I made it.~~ Meeting my goal was the perfect end

to the summer

PRACTICE AND APPLY

Revise Your Own Personal Narrative

1. Read your draft aloud or have your partner read it to you. Listen to the way the words flow. How does it sound?

2. Add vivid words that describe.

3. Use the notes from your peer conference to help you revise your draft.

4. Add an interesting title that will "grab" your reader's interest.

Checklist ✓

Revising

- **Does your story suit your purpose and audience?**

- **Did you describe a personal experience?**

- **Do you need to elaborate on any part of your narrative?**

- **Did you use colorful, exact words to describe the experience and your feelings about it?**

- **Did you use time-order words to tell when the events occurred?**

- **Do your sentences flow smoothly when read aloud?**

- **Did you add an interesting title?**

Writing PROCESS

Proofread/Edit

After you have revised your personal narrative, you will need to proofread and edit it to find and correct any errors in mechanics, grammar and usage, and spelling.

STRATEGIES FOR PROOFREADING

- **Reread your revised paper several times.** Each time you read, look for a different type of error. This will give you a better chance of catching your mistakes.

- **Reread for mechanics and usage.** Make sure you have used a capital letter to begin every sentence and the correct punctuation at the end of each sentence.

- **Check for commas.** Make sure you use a comma and the word *and*, *but*, or *or* to make compound sentences.

- **Check for spelling errors by reading your paper from the last word to the first word.** You will be able to concentrate on the spelling of the words instead of on the story.

Spelling

When choosing *ei* or *ie*, remember that *i* comes before *e*, as in *friend*, except after *c*, as in *receive*, or when sounded like /ā/, as in *neighbor* or *weigh*.

REVIEW THE RULES

GRAMMAR

- A compound sentence joins two complete sentences by using a comma and the words *and*, *but*, or *or*.

MECHANICS

- Every sentence begins with a capital letter.

- A declarative sentence ends with a period.

- An interrogative sentence ends with a question mark.

- An imperative sentence ends with a period.

- An exclamatory sentence ends with an exclamation mark.

- A run-on sentence joins together two or more sentences that should be written separately.

Go to pages 138–169 to review other rules.

Look at the proofreading corrections made on the draft below. What does the symbol ⊙ mean? Why does the writer use it to end the last sentence?

PREWRITE

DRAFT

REVISE

PROOFREAD

PUBLISH

PROOFREAD

The Perfect Summer Ending

                          Camp Wilderness ⌐
Last summer, I went to ~~camp.~~ I go to the same
           , but   ^   (SP) different
camp every year. Last summer was ~~diffrent.~~

That was the summer I decided to swim across

Lake Wonder.
                                 First,
      I knew it wouldn't be easy. I made a plan to meet
        Next,
my goal. I asked the camp counselors to help me
  Then,   shimmering blue
train. After three weeks of training in and out of the ^
I finally felt ready # (SP) friends
water, ~~it was time.~~ My ~~freinds~~ came to cheer me on

as I jumped in and began to swim. My sister Linda

even videotaped the event ⊙≡ one of the counselors

rowed in a boat next to me for safety. ~~It wasn't easy,~~
How excited I was when I made it across the lake!
~~but I made it.~~ Meeting my goal was the perfect end
         ^
to the summer⊙

Checklist ✓
Proofreading

- Did you indent each paragraph?

- Did you group sentences about the same idea into a paragraph?

- Did you check the spelling of difficult words?

- Did you use a capital letter to begin every sentence and the correct punctuation at the end of each sentence?

- Did you combine any sentences or correct run-on sentences?

PRACTICE AND APPLY

Proofread Your Own Personal Narrative

1. Find and correct misspelled words.

2. Include the correct ending punctuation for each kind of sentence.

3. Make sure you use a comma and the words *and*, *but*, or *or* to join compound sentences.

4. Know the meaning of each word you use.

PROOFREADING MARKS

#	new paragraph
^	add
⌐	take out
≡	Make a capital letter.
/	Make a small letter.
(SP)	Check the spelling.
⊙	Add a period.

Writing PROCESS

Publish

The last step before publishing your piece is to review your writing one last time. Use a checklist to help you keep track of what you have reviewed.

✓ Self-Check Personal Narrative

- ❏ What was my purpose? Did I describe a personal experience?
- ❏ Did I choose a topic that will interest my audience?
- ❏ Did I include a good title?
- ❏ Did I use a variety of sentences? Do my sentences flow together?
- ❏ Did I end each type of sentence with the correct punctuation?
- ❏ Did I correctly use compound sentences?
- ❏ Did I use time-order words to show the sequence of events?
- ❏ Did I include enough specific details so that the reader can easily visualize my experience?
- ❏ Did I proofread and correct all errors?

The writer used the checklist to review his personal narrative. Read "The Perfect Summer Ending" and discuss the writer's published piece with a small group. Do you think it was ready to publish? Why do you think so?

24

The Perfect Summer Ending

by Brad Lewis

Last summer, I went to Camp Wilderness. I go to the same camp every year, but last summer was different. That was the summer I decided to swim across Lake Wonder. I knew it wouldn't be easy.

First, I made a plan to meet my goal. Next, I asked the camp counselors to help me train. Then, after three weeks of training in and out of the shimmering blue water, I finally felt ready.

My friends came to cheer me on as I jumped in and began to swim. My sister Linda even videotaped the event. One of the counselors rowed in a boat next to me for safety. How excited I was when I made it across the lake! Meeting my goal was the perfect end to the summer.

PRACTICE AND APPLY

Publish Your Own Personal Narrative

1. Check your revised draft one more time.

2. Make a neat, final copy.

3. Add a border, pictures, or a cover to your story.

4. Send your story to your school newspaper.

TECHNOLOGY

Does your school have a Web site? Use your school's technology resources to publish your work on the Internet.

Personal Narrative

Score	Description
4 **Excellent**	■ tells an entertaining story about a personal experience and includes thoughts and feelings ■ presents details in an easy-to-follow sequence ■ always uses the first person and clearly expresses feelings ■ includes a strong beginning, middle, and end ■ uses a variety of time-order words ■ varies types and lengths of sentences ■ is free or almost free of errors
3 **Good**	■ tells about a personal experience and includes some thoughts and feelings ■ presents details in the correct order ■ mostly uses the first person and expresses feelings ■ uses some time-order words ■ uses both simple and compound sentences ■ has minor errors that do not confuse the reader
2 **Fair**	■ tells about a personal experience but often loses focus ■ includes events told out of order ■ does not always use the first person and expresses few feelings ■ lacks time-order words ■ uses only simple sentences ■ makes frequent errors that confuse the reader
1 **Unsatisfactory**	■ does not share a personal experience and is not focused or entertaining ■ tells events out of order and is confusing ■ does not use first person and does not express feelings ■ does not use time-order words ■ sentences are choppy or run together ■ makes serious and repeated errors

Go to www.macmillanmh.com for a 6-Point Student Writing Rubric.

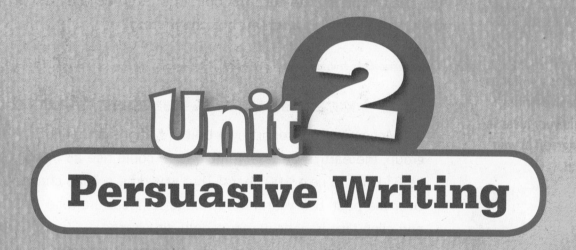

Unit 2
Persuasive Writing

Persuasive Writing

When you try to get people to agree with your point of view, you are trying to *persuade* them. Persuasive writing tries to persuade an audience to adopt the writer's opinion. Sometimes it even tries to persuade people to take action.

Learning from Writers

Read the following examples of persuasive writing. As you read, look for the authors' opinions. How do they make their arguments? Is each author convincing?

THINK AND WRITE

Purpose

Why does a writer use persuasive writing? Explain your ideas in a paragraph in your journal.

The Forecast: A Warmer World

According to a report by a United Nations scientific group, the earth's average temperature could rise as much as 6° F in the next 100 years! That would be a huge change. Over the past 100 years, the average temperature rose 1° F, and even that is considered to be a big change.

Even a small rise in the earth's temperature could have a big impact. The U.N. scientists predict that over the next century, polar ice caps and glaciers could melt, raising ocean levels as much as three feet. Low-lying land along seacoasts and in river basins could flood. Entire islands in the Pacific could be under water. Many people could have to move to higher ground.

Global warming could also make weather less predictable, with extreme heat and cold, drought and more violent storms. Rainfall patterns could change. Some farm areas could be unable to grow crops.

What can we do? Most nations have taken small steps to control the release of gases that trap heat. Everyone agrees that stronger measures are needed. Scientists now know global warming can't be ignored much longer.

—from "The Forecast: A Warmer World," in *Time for Kids*

94 East 8th Street
Clover, MO 63805
May 17, 20__

Division Publishing Company
886 Third Avenue
New York, NY 10022

Dear Mr. Cisneros:

    I am writing you on behalf of the fifth-grade classes at the Whitney School. Everyone here loves your books, and in a recent student vote, you were chosen Author of the Year.

    Our language arts teacher noticed that you are on a lecture tour and will be speaking in Kansas City on June 21. The town of Clover is nearby, and I would like to invite you to stop here on your way to Kansas City. Everyone would be delighted if you could come and speak on any subject.

    Please let me know if you will be able to speak so that we can make arrangements for your stay.

Sincerely yours,
Tracy Dell

PRACTICE AND APPLY

Thinking Like a Reader

1. List the reasons that the author of "The Forecast: A Warmer World" is concerned about global warming.

2. Read Tracy Dell's letter again. Why does she want Mr. Cisneros to come to her school?

Thinking Like a Writer

3. How does the author of "The Forecast: A Warmer World" persuade the audience to agree with his opinion?

4. Where does Tracy place her strongest argument? Do you think it will persuade Mr. Cisneros to speak at her school? Why?

5. Reading Across Texts Compare the two literature models. Which one is more convincing? Why?

Features of Persuasive Writing

GUIDELINES

Persuasive writing states the opinion of the writer and attempts to influence an audience to agree with that opinion. Persuasive writing:

▶ clearly **states an opinion** on a specific topic.

▶ uses **convincing reasons** and arguments.

▶ organizes reasons in a **logical order**.

▶ usually saves the **strongest argument for last**.

▶ includes **opinion words**.

▶ An Opinion

Reread "The Forecast: A Warmer World" on page 28. What is the author's opinion about global warming?

> Scientists now know global warming can't be ignored much longer.

This persuasive conclusion summarizes the author's opinion about global warming.

▶ Convincing Reasons

The author states that global warming could cause flooding. What reasons are listed to convince the reader that the floods would be harmful?

> Low-lying land along seacoasts and in river basins could flood. Entire islands in the Pacific could be under water. Many people could have to move to higher ground.

The author gives a list of ways that flooding would hurt human beings and other species.

▶ Logical Order

To make a clear argument, it is important to give reasons or details in a logical order. Reread the first paragraph of "The Forecast: A Warmer World." Why are the details listed in this order? Does the writer begin with a strong lead?

> According to a report by a United Nations scientific group, the earth's average temperature could rise as much as 6° F in the next 100 years! That would be a huge change. Over the past 100 years, the average temperature rose 1° F, and even that is considered to be a big change.

The author begins with a strong lead. He uses the example of the 1° F change to show the impact of a 6° F change.

▶ Strongest Argument Last

The author's last argument is meant to leave a strong impression on the reader. This makes it a strong ending.

> Global warming could also make weather less predictable, with extreme heat and cold, drought and more violent storms.

The author's final argument is strong because it lists changes that would directly affect people.

▶ Opinion Words

The author uses opinion words to appeal to the way an audience thinks and feels.

> Everyone agrees that stronger measures are needed.

The author uses the words *Everyone agrees* to persuade the audience to adopt his point of view.

PRACTICE AND APPLY

Create a Features Chart

1. List the features of good persuasive writing.
2. Reread Tracy Dell's letter on page 29.
3. What is Tracy's most persuasive argument?
4. Write one example in Tracy's letter for three of the five features of a personal narrative.

Features	Examples

Prewrite

Persuasive writing presents a writer's opinion about a topic and tries to persuade an audience to agree with that opinion. Persuasive writing may also influence an audience to take a certain plan of action.

Purpose and Audience

The purpose of persuasive writing is to persuade your reader to adopt your opinion. In persuasive writing, you must use convincing reasons and language that will persuade your audience to agree with your point of view.

When planning a persuasive letter, for example, you need to think about your reader. What is his or her opinion about your topic? What will you need to say to get your audience to think as you do?

Choose a Topic

Start by **brainstorming** a list of issues or topics that you feel strongly about. Choose the issue most important to you.

Next, **explore ideas** by making a list of at least three reasons that support your opinion. For each reason, give facts and opinions to support it. Later, you will put your reasons in a logical order.

THINK AND WRITE

Audience
How will your audience's opinion about your topic influence the way you plan and write your persuasive letter? Write your ideas in your journal.

Here is my list of reasons that support my opinion.

Why We Should Clean Up the Park

A clean park will be good for business.
(Shoppers will like coming to the area.)
Litter looks bad.
Trash is not good for the environment.
Trash causes disease.
Cleaning up would be fun.
Cleaning up the park would make our community proud.
Cleaning up would help trash collectors.
Store owners and businesses should help.

Organize • Reasons and Explanations

To plan your persuasive letter, you need to include **facts** and **opinions** that support your position. A fact can be proved to be true. An opinion cannot. As you write your reasons and explain them, jot down whether each reason is a fact or an opinion. Which ideas from her list did the writer leave out?

REASON-AND-EXPLANATION CHART

Position Statement:
Our community park should be cleaned up.   opinion

Reason: A clean park will be good for business.   opinion

Explanation: Shoppers will come to the area.   opinion

Reason: Litter is harmful to the environment.   fact

Explanation: Litter can pollute the water.   fact

Reason: Cleaning up the park would be a good experience.   opinion

Explanation: It's fun to work together with your friends.   opinion

Reason: Cleaning up the park will build community pride.   opinion

Explanation: People take care of their community when they are proud of it.   not sure

Conclusion: Business owners should help clean up the park.   opinion

Checklist ✔

Prewriting

- **Did you think about your purpose and audience?**

- **Did you choose an issue and decide on your position?**

- **Did you list reasons and explanations that support your opinion?**

- **Did you organize your reasons in a chart?**

- **Did you arrange your reasons in a logical order?**

- **Do you need to find facts or do any research?**

PRACTICE AND APPLY

Plan Your Own Persuasive Writing

1. Think about your purpose and audience.

2. Brainstorm a list of topics and choose one.

3. Use the reason-and-explanation chart to organize your ideas.

Prewrite • Research and Inquiry

▶ Writer's Resources

You may need to do research to support your position in your persuasive letter. First, make a list of questions that your audience might have about your topic. Then decide which resources you will need to answer your questions.

What Else Do I Need to Know?	Where Can I Find the Information?
What conditions affect where people shop?	Interview shopkeepers and community leaders.
What problems does litter create in the environment?	Look in reference and other nonfiction books, and search the Internet.

▶ Use Parts of a Book

Nonfiction books are useful resouces for a writer. These books have different parts to help you find information. In the front of the book, the **title page** tells you the book's title, author, and publisher. The **copyright page** tells you the year the book was published. The **table of contents** lists the titles of the chapters or main sections and the page number on which each begins. In the back of the book, an **index** lists all the topics in the book in alphabetical order.

INDEX

Litter
clean-up campaigns, 148
effects on environment, 122–123
water pollution, 139

STRATEGIES FOR USING PARTS OF A BOOK

- Check the copyright page to make sure the information is current.

- Check to see if the table of contents contains the type of information you are looking for.

- If the table of contents is too general, look at the index for specific topics.

Writing PROCESS

► Choose Reference Sources

It is important to think carefully about your topic when choosing reference sources. If you are writing about a local issue, you might want to ask your community leaders for information. If you need recent information to support facts and opinions, use the *Readers' Guide to Periodical Literature* to find current magazine or newspaper articles. The Internet can also help you find information to support your opinion or position.

► Use Your Research

After completing your research, add any new facts to your reason-and-explanation chart. This writer found information about neighborhood clean-up programs. She also found more details about litter and the environment. How did she change her chart?

PREWRITE

DRAFT

REVISE

PROOFREAD

PUBLISH

Reason: A clean park will be good for business.   opinion
I've read that people spend more time in places that are surrounded by trees, plants, and grass.   fact
Explanation: Shoppers will come to the area.   opinion
Cleaning up will help businesses near the park.   opinion

Reason: Litter is harmful to the environment.   fact

Explanation: Litter can pollute the water.   fact
People, animals, and plants are healthier in unpoluted areas.   fact

PRACTICE AND APPLY

Review Your Plan

1. Look at your reason-and-explanation chart.

2. Jot down questions a reader might ask about the ideas you listed in your chart.

3. Identify the resources you will need to find answers to your questions.

4. Add new facts that you gather to your chart.

Checklist ✓

Research and Inquiry

■ Did you list questions a reader might have?

■ Did you identify possible references?

■ Did you take notes and list your sources?

Draft

Before you begin writing your persuasive letter, review the chart you made. Think about writing a paragraph for each reason you listed. Include details, especially facts, that support each reason. Arrange your reasons in a logical order. Save your strongest reason for last.

Main idea for first paragraph: My position on cleaning up the park

REASON-AND-EXPLANATION CHART

Position Statement:
Our community park should be cleaned up.   opinion

Reason: ~~A clean park will be good for business.~~   opinion
I've read that people spend more time in places
that are surrounded by trees, plants, and grass.   fact
Explanation: ~~Shoppers will come to the area.~~   opinion
Cleaning up will help businesses near
the park.   opinion

This reason is weak: I'll drop this.

Reason: Litter is harmful to the environment.   fact

Explanation: Litter can pollute the water.   fact
People, animals, and plants are healthier
in unpoluted areas.   fact

Reason: Cleaning up the park would be a
good experience.   opinion

Explanation: It's fun to work together with
your friends.   opinion

Reason: Cleaning up the park will build
community pride.   opinion

Explanation: People take care of their
community when they are proud of it.   ~~not sure~~
opinion

Conclusion: Business owners should help
clean up the park.   opinion

Main idea for the last paragraph before my conclusion: My strongest reason for cleaning up the park.

✓ Checklist

Drafting

- Remember purpose and audience. Will your letter persuade your audience?

- Did you state your position clearly?

- Did you include facts and opinions to support your reasons?

- Did you save your strongest argument for last?

- Did you end with a logical conclusion?

Look at the way this writer used the ideas in her reason-and-explanation chart to write a first draft.

DRAFT

Dear mr. Stanley

There is a lot of litter in Midtown Park. We students are hoping you can help us chang that for three reasons.

[*Opinion is clearly stated.*

I've read that people spend more time in places that are surrounded by trees, plants, and grass. Since there are stores next to the park, it would help business to clean up the land.

[*First reason is stated and supported by opinion.*

Also, litter is harmful to the environment. People, animals, and plants are healthier in unpoluted areas.

[*Second reason is stated and backed up by fact.*

Community pride is another good reason to help. When citizens work together, they feel pride and take care of their community

[*Third and strongest reason is stated and supported by opinion.*

If you don't mind, a volunteer will be calling soon to see if you can donate some materials. Remember: Your customers are depending on you to help. Your community is also depending on you to help.

Sincerly

Patricia Perez

PRACTICE AND APPLY

Draft Your Own Persuasive Letter

1. Review your prewriting chart.
2. State your position at the beginning of the letter.
3. Give your reasons in a logical order.

TECHNOLOGY

Be sure that your reasons are written in a logical order with the strongest one last. If not, use the cut-and-paste features on your computer to rearrange sentences or paragraphs in the order that will be most convincing to your audience.

Revise

Elaborate

One way to improve your writing is to elaborate. When you elaborate, you add important facts, reasons, opinions, and details that might be missing from your writing. When you revise your persuasive letter, you may need to include more reasons or details to prove your point. The facts and details that this writer added make her arguments more convincing.

> ~Studies show~ I've read that people spend more time in places ^clean downtown areas^
>
> that are surrounded by trees, plants, and grass.

The writer changed her wording to make her statement more forceful. She also added specific information to influence her reader.

> your
> Since there are stores next to the park, it would ^is^
> your
> ^help~ business to clean up the land.

Word Choice

When you use persuasive writing, it is important to understand how the words you choose can influence your audience. In a persuasive letter, **opinion words** help make your statements more convincing.

> Everyone knows that
> ^People, animals, and plants are healthier in
>
> unpoluted areas.
> the best
> Community pride is ~another good~ reason to help.

OPINION WORDS

I believe

I think

in my opinion

obviously

everyone

no one

ought

should

most

best

least

Better Sentences

As you continue to revise your draft, check your sentences to make sure they fit together well. Read the sentences aloud. Have you combined sentences that repeat the same idea about two different nouns? By combining sentences with similar information about two different nouns, you can avoid writing short, choppy sentences.

Remember: Your customers are depending on you to help.

Your community is also depending on you to help.

Remember: Your customers and community are depending on you to help.

PRACTICE AND APPLY

Revise Your Own Persuasive Letter

1. Add facts and opinions to explain your reasons and make them more convincing.

2. Include opinion words that will influence your audience to accept your position.

3. Make sure that each paragraph introduces a new reason to support your argument.

4. **Grammar** Should you combine sentences that repeat the same idea about two different nouns?

TECHNOLOGY

Find out if your classmates know how to use the automatic letter-formatting function or other word-processing shortcuts. Ask them to explain and demonstrate what they know.

Revise • Peer Conferencing

Now that you have made your best first effort, exchange drafts with a partner. Your partner may have new ideas for making your letter more interesting and persuasive.

Writing PROCESS

> You need an opening that gets the reader's attention.

> Interesting! Could you tell me more about your research?

> Time-order and opinion words could make your ideas flow better.

> Good point!

> What do you need? Be specific.

Dear mr. Stanley

There is a lot of litter in Midtown Park. We students are hoping you can help us chang that for three reasons.

I've read that people spend more time in places that are surrounded by trees, plants, and grass. Since there are stores next to the park, it would help business to clean up the land.

Also, litter is harmful to the environment. People, animals, and plants are healthier in unpoluted areas.

Community pride is another good reason to help. When citizens work together, they feel pride and take care of their community

If you don't mind, a volunteer will be calling soon to see if you can donate some materials. Remember: Your customers are depending on you to help. Your community is also depending on you to help.

Sincerly

Patricia Perez

TiP!

Conferencing for the Reader

- Are the features of persuasive writing included in your partner's letter?
  - writer's opinion
  - convincing reasons
  - opinion words
  - reasons presented in a logical order
  - strongest argument last
- Discuss what you like about your partner's writing as well as what needs revising.

When you revise your persuasive letter, think about your partner's suggestions. This writer used her partner's ideas to correct and improve several parts of her letter.

REVISE

Dear mr. Stanley

Have you noticed the
~~There is a lot of~~ litter in Midtown Park. We students are

hoping you can help us chang that for three reasons.

First, studies show   clean downtown areas
~~I've read~~ that people spend more time in ~~places~~

that are surrounded by trees, plants, and grass.

your   is   your
Since ~~there are~~ stores next to the park, it would help

business to clean up the land.

Second   Everyone knows that
Also, litter is harmful to the environment. People,

animals, and plants are healthier in unpoluted areas.

Third,   the best
Community pride is ~~another good~~ reason to help.

When citizens work together, they feel pride and take

care of their community

If you don't mind, a volunteer will be calling soon to
shovels, trash cans, gloves, and other
see if you can donate ~~some~~ materials. Remember: Your
and community
customers are depending on you to help. ~~Your~~

~~community is also depending on you to help.~~

Sincerly

Patricia Perez

Checklist ✓

Revising

- Have you made your position clear?

- Will your reasons persuade your audience to agree with you?

- Have you included facts and opinions?

- Did you include opinion words to make your arguments stronger?

- Did you use different kinds of sentences in each paragraph?

- Is your conclusion persuasive and logical?

PRACTICE AND APPLY

Revise Your Own Persuasive Letter

1. Use the notes from your peer conference.

2. Take out unnecessary information from your draft.

3. Check that you have used the correct letter form.

Proofread/Edit

Once you have revised your persuasive letter, you will need to proofread and edit it to find and correct any errors in mechanics, grammar and usage, and spelling.

STRATEGIES FOR PROOFREADING

Read your revised letter more than once. Look for a different kind of error each time you read. Remember: It is easier to concentrate on one kind of error at a time.

- **Check for correct capitalization in each part of your letter.** Each name and title before it, greeting, and closing of a letter must begin with a capital letter.

- **Check for correct punctuation in each part of your letter.** Be sure that you have used a colon after your greeting and a comma after the last word in your closing.

- **Check for spelling mistakes.** Read slowly and carefully rather than reading at your normal rate.

Spelling

When the /j/ sound is spelled *g*, *g* is always followed by *e*, *i*, or *y*, as in the word *change*.

REVIEW THE RULES

GRAMMAR

- **Sentences** with similar information about two different nouns **may be combined.** Use the **conjunction** *and* or *or* to join nouns in a sentence.

MECHANICS

- The **greeting** and the **closing** of a letter must begin with a **capital letter**.

- A **colon** follows the **greeting** in a business letter.

- A **comma** follows the last word in the **closing** of a letter.

- In the inside address, a **comma** separates the **name of a city and state** and the **day and year** in a date.

Go to pages 138–169 to review other rules.

Notice the proofreading marks on the draft below. What does the ∽ symbol mean? Why does the writer replace *places* with *clean downtown areas*?

PROOFREAD

Dear mr. Stanley:

¶ Have you noticed the

~~There is a lot of~~ litter in Midtown Park. We students are

change
hoping you can help us chang that for three reasons.

First, studies show

clean downtown areas
~~I've read~~ that people spend more time in ~~places~~

that are surrounded by trees, plants, and grass.

your   is   your
Since ~~there are~~ stores next to the park, it would help

business to clean up the land.

Second

Everyone knows that
~~Also,~~ litter is harmful to the environment. People,

unpolluted
animals, and plants are healthier in ~~unpoluted~~ areas.

Third,   the best
Community pride is ~~another good~~ reason to help.

When citizens work together, they feel pride and take

care of their community⊙

If you don't mind, a volunteer will be calling soon to

shovels, trash cans, gloves, and other
see if you can donate ~~some~~ materials. Remember: Your

and community
customers are depending on you to help. ~~Your~~

~~community is also depending on you to help.~~

Sincerely
Sincerly,

Patricia Perez

Checklist ✓

Proofreading

- Did you use correct letter capitalization and punctuation?

- Did you use correct end punctuation?

- Did you use the correct form for a business letter and indent your letter correctly?

- Did you spell all the words correctly?

PROOFREADING MARKS

⌗ new paragraph

∧ add

∽ take out

≡ Make a capital letter.

/ Make a small letter.

SP Check the spelling.

⊙ Add a period.

PRACTICE AND APPLY

Proofread Your Own Persuasive Letter

1. Correct spelling mistakes.

2. Check for correct letter form, including capitalization, punctuation, and formatting.

3. Use the Proofreading Checklist.

Publish

Review your persuasive letter one more time to see if you are ready to publish it. Follow the checklist below to help you decide if your work is ready to share.

✓ Self-Check   Persuasive Letter

- ❑ Did I make my position clear at the beginning of my letter?
- ❑ Did I put my reasons in a logical order with the strongest argument last?
- ❑ Who is my reader? Will my arguments be convincing to him or her?
- ❑ Did I get my reader's interest at the beginning of my letter and end with a persuasive conclusion?
- ❑ Did I include enough facts to support my reasons?
- ❑ Did I vary my sentences so they fit together well?
- ❑ Did I use opinion words to express my views and sway my audience?
- ❑ Did I use correct capitalization for proper nouns?
- ❑ Did I proofread for correct letter punctuation and form?
- ❑ Did I correct all errors?

The writer used the checklist to make sure her letter was her best work. Read her letter. Discuss the writer's purpose and the strategies she used to achieve it. Do you think the letter is convincing? Give reasons for your opinion.

PREWRITE

DRAFT

REVISE

PROOFREAD

PUBLISH

Park Ridge School
4617 Cedar Drive
Bellaire, TX 77401
November 12, 20—

Central Hardware Company
3144 Bell Boulevard
Bellaire, TX 77401

Dear Mr. Stanley:

Have you noticed the litter in Midtown Park? We students are hoping you can help us change that for three reasons.

First, studies show that people spend more time in clean downtown areas that are surrounded by trees, plants, and grass. Since your store is next to the park, it would help your business to clean up the land.

Second, litter is harmful to the environment. Everyone knows that people, animals, and plants are healthier in unpolluted areas.

Third, community pride is the best reason to help. When citizens work together, they feel pride and take care of their community.

If you don't mind, a volunteer will be calling soon to see if you can donate shovels, trash cans, gloves, and other materials. Remember: Your customers and community are depending on you to help.

Sincerely,

Patricia Perez

TECHNOLOGY

Learn to use your computer and printer to address an envelope. Select the envelope formatting option and type in the receiver's address and your return address. Ask someone to help you position the envelope in the printer.

PRACTICE AND APPLY

Publish Your Own Persuasive Letter

1. Check your revised draft one last time.

2. Make a neat, final copy of your draft.

3. Address an envelope and add your return address.

Persuasive Writing

Score	Description
4 Excellent	■ presents a focused, clear opinion with supporting details ■ presents reasons in a logical order, with strongest reason last ■ encourages readers with a strong opinion and personal tone ■ uses many well-chosen opinion words ■ uses a variety of sentence types ■ is free or almost free of errors
3 Good	■ presents a clear opinion with supporting details ■ presents reasons for an opinion in a logical order ■ makes a strong attempt at using a personal tone to present opinions ■ uses several well-chosen opinion words ■ uses a variety of sentence types ■ has minor errors that do not confuse the reader
2 Fair	■ attempts to present an opinion, but supporting details are few or weak ■ presents reasons for the opinion, but not in the most logical order ■ does not communicate a personal opinion and uses little personal tone ■ uses only one or two opinion words ■ sentences are choppy or run together ■ makes frequent errors that confuse the reader
1 Unsatisfactory	■ does not present an opinion ■ misses reasons or presents them in a confusing order ■ lacks any personal tone that might engage the reader ■ does not use opinion words ■ uses run-on sentences and sentence fragments ■ makes serious and repeated errors

Go to www.macmillanmh.com for a 6-Point Student Writing Rubric.

Unit 3

Fictional Narrative: A Story

Fictional Narrative: A Story

Have you ever written a story that you created yourself? If so, your story probably had a setting, characters, and a plot with a problem that is solved at the end. In some ways, a story is like a personal narrative. However, a story is a work of fiction. It is a narrative that a writer creates from his or her imagination. Like a personal narrative, the main purpose of a fictional narrative is to entertain an audience.

Learning from Writers

Read the following examples of fictional narrative. Why do you think the authors wrote these stories? As you read, look for phrases that build excitement or add suspense.

THINK AND WRITE

Purpose

Why do you think people write and tell stories? Write your ideas in your journal.

A New Coach

Back in class, Mariah felt she couldn't stand the suspense any longer. Game time was only twenty minutes away. Just as she was about to ask if anybody had been chosen to play, Brandon beat her to it. He would, she thought. He's so smart.

"Mrs. Floyd, are we in the game today?"

"I was beginning to wonder if anybody was interested," Mrs. Floyd answered in a teasing voice.

The class groaned. Mariah let out a low "Aw, no."

Mrs. Floyd went on. "We have three players from our room—Cynthia, Brandon, and Nikki."

Mariah felt everybody's eyes on her. Her stomach felt weak. . . . She heard the cheers for her classmates. But she was so stunned by not having been chosen, she didn't pay any attention to what else her teacher was saying.

"Even though she's small, she has what in volleyball is called good hands. She hits and passes well. . . . She moves fast and many times jumps almost as high as she is tall. A hard worker, one hundred percent dedicated to the game, the fifth grade coach, Mariah Metcalf, Room 111!"

The room exploded with cheers. Mariah couldn't believe it. Coach of all fifth grade rooms!

—Mildred Pitts Walter, from *Mariah Loves Rock*

A Narrow Escape

Each wave smashing against the cliffs threw showers of spray into the air. The two children scrambling across the slippery rocks were soaked by the morning spray.

"I can see it now!" shouted Jenny, straining to be heard above the roar of the ocean. She clambered down the steep rock into a shallow pool that was sheltered from the raging sea. Her brother Ben followed.

"Are the flashlights still working?" he asked. Two beams of light pierced the gloom. "Then, let's go," said Ben. They waded into the small opening.

Hidden behind a ridge in the wall was a narrow gap. The children squeezed into a tight, twisty passage of rock.

Ben and Jenny rushed along the passage, finally emerging on the other side. "We made it before high tide," yelled Jenny.

"We're lucky, Sis," Ben smiled.

—Iris Begay

PRACTICE AND APPLY

Thinking Like a Reader

1. Who is the main character in "A New Coach"?

2. What is the setting in "A Narrow Escape"?

Thinking Like a Writer

3. How did the author of "A New Coach" use dialogue to describe the characters?

4. What words did the author of "A Narrow Escape" use to help you picture the setting?

5. **Reading Across Texts** Compare the two literature models. Write about the problem in each model and how it is solved at the end.

Features of a Story

GUIDELINES

A story is a fictional narrative that a writer creates from his or her imagination. A good story:

▶ has an interesting **beginning**, **middle**, and **end**.

▶ describes a **setting**, telling when and where a story takes place.

▶ has **characters** that move the action along.

▶ has a **plot** with a problem that is solved at the end.

▶ often uses **dialogue**.

▶ Beginning, Middle, and End

Reread "A New Coach" on page 48. Notice the way the story begins and ends.

> Back in class, Mariah felt she couldn't stand the suspense any longer. . . .
>
> The room exploded with cheers. Mariah couldn't believe it. Coach of all the fifth grade rooms!

Think about the way the author builds excitement and suspense. Notice that the exclamation makes you realize how happy Mariah felt at the end. How does the ending let you know what happens?

▶ Setting

Setting is an important part of "A New Coach." How do the following sentences help you understand where and when the story takes place?

> Back in class, Mariah felt she couldn't stand the suspense any longer. Game time was only twenty minutes away.

This sentence explains that the characters are in class anxiously waiting for a sporting event to begin. The story also takes place in the present.

▶ Characters

The thoughts, words, and deeds of characters help move the action of the story along. The sentences below describe the actions of two characters.

> Just as she was about to ask if anybody had been chosen to play, Brandon beat her to it. He would, she thought. He's so smart.

What do you learn about Brandon from his action? Notice that Mariah's thoughts about him help you to see the character. They also help describe Mariah.

▶ Plot

A good story has a strong plot, or sequence of events, that introduces a problem that is solved at the end.

> But she was so stunned by not having been chosen, she didn't pay any attention to what else her teacher was saying.

How does the sentence show you the story's problem?

▶ Dialogue

Read the teacher's words at the end of "A New Coach."

> "A hard worker, one hundred percent dedicated to the game, the fifth grade coach, Mariah Metcalf, Room 111!"

How does the dialogue tell you that the problem is solved?

PRACTICE AND APPLY

Create a Story Map

1. List the features of writing a good story.
2. Reread "A Narrow Escape" by Iris Begay on page 49.
3. How does the writer use dialogue to tell her story?
4. Fill in the story map.
5. Write how the problem is solved at the end.

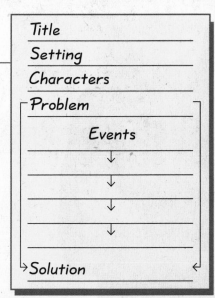

Prewrite

A fictional narrative comes from the writer's imagination. A good story has a strong setting, characters, and a plot, or series of events. At the center of the plot is a problem, or conflict, that the main character tries to solve by the end of the story.

Purpose and Audience

The purpose of writing a story is to use your imagination to entertain your readers, or audience.

Before writing, think about the members of your audience. Who will be reading or listening to your story? Think about the kind of story that will amuse them. What will make them smile? What will amaze them?

Choose a Topic

Start by **brainstorming** a list of possible topics. You might think about experiences that have happened to someone you know, or just use your imagination. Then choose the topic that you feel will make the most interesting story for your audience.

After choosing a topic, **explore ideas** by making a list of events of the plot. Your events will need to include a problem and its solution. Also, list characters and a setting. Later, you will organize your ideas.

THINK AND WRITE

Audience

How will your audience affect the way you plan and write your story? Write your ideas in your journal.

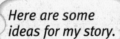
Here are some ideas for my story.

My Story About Boy Inventor

Boy likes to experiment with
    chemistry set.
Boy's mother's flowers die.
Boy tries to find answer to
    why flowers die.
Boy solves problem with
    secret formula.
Boy wins a prize.
Boy invents new things.

Writing PROCESS

Organize • Story Elements

The characters, setting, and plot events depend on one another to make a complete story. To put all the "pieces" of a story together, you can use a story map. Not all your ideas may be needed to tell your story. What ideas from her list did this writer leave out of her story map?

PREWRITE

DRAFT

REVISE

PROOFREAD

PUBLISH

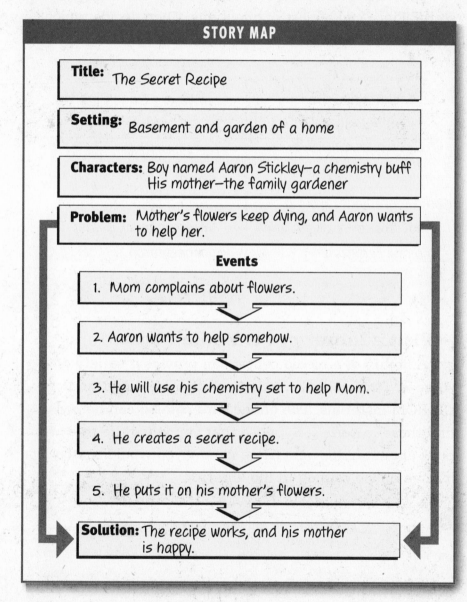

STORY MAP

Title: The Secret Recipe

Setting: Basement and garden of a home

Characters: Boy named Aaron Stickley—a chemistry buff
His mother—the family gardener

Problem: Mother's flowers keep dying, and Aaron wants to help her.

Events

1. Mom complains about flowers.

2. Aaron wants to help somehow.

3. He will use his chemistry set to help Mom.

4. He creates a secret recipe.

5. He puts it on his mother's flowers.

Solution: The recipe works, and his mother is happy.

PRACTICE AND APPLY

Plan Your Own Story

1. Think about your purpose and audience.

2. Brainstorm ideas for a topic, and choose one.

3. Explore ideas for characters, setting, and events.

4. Use the story map to organize your ideas.

Checklist ✓

Prewriting

- Did you think about your purpose and audience?

- Did you choose a good topic and explore ideas?

- Did you think about the characters and setting of your story?

- Did you organize your ideas in a story map?

- Have you checked the order of events and arranged them according to a beginning, a middle, and an end?

- Do you need to do any research?

Writing PROCESS

Prewrite • Research and Inquiry

▶ Writer's Resources

You may have to do research to get more information for your fictional narrative. For example, what do you need to know about wildflowers or chemistry to write your story? First, make a list of questions. Then decide which resources you will need in order to answer them.

What Else Do I Need to Know?	Where Can I Find the Information?
What are some different kinds of flowers?	Visit a library or a media center to do research.
Could ingredients from a chemistry set really be used to make fertilizer?	Look in a card catalog for information, or do an online search.

▶ Visit a Library or a Media Center

A library or a media center can provide a variety of sources, such as books, videos, audio recordings, and CD-ROM materials. The online card catalog can help you find these materials. Suppose that you knew the title of a book about wildflowers. Here is how you would search for it in an online catalog in the library.

Welcome to the Online Public Access Catalog
SEARCH
Press A to search by AUTHOR'S NAME
Press B to search by TITLE
Press C to search by SUBJECT
Press D to search for items with a particular KEYWORD or words anywhere in the author's name, title, or subject
Press E to enter Advanced Search Mode
Press F to search by CALL NUMBER
Press G for Other Search Options
Press A-G or a Command Key

TITLE SEARCH: A Book of Wildflowers
Kelvin, P.C. — A Book of Wildflowers
CALL NUMBER: J582.13
AUTHOR: Kelvin, P.C.
TITLE: A Book of Wildflowers by P.C. Kelvin, illustrated by Joyce Wong
PUBLISHED: New York: Voyager Press ©1999
PAGING: 30p.; ill. (col.); 23 cm.
ANNOTATION: An introduction to the many varieties of wildflowers
LIBRARY HOLDINGS at: Mainview Lib.
Call Number J582.13   ON SHELF

▶ Use a Card Catalog

As you know, when visiting the library, you can use the card catalog to find books that will help you in doing research for your story. These cards can be found in drawers or online. Each library book usually has three cards in the card catalog: the author card, the title card, and the subject card. Each of these cards gives the same information about the book, but in a different order.

You use the author card when you know the author of the book but not the title. You use the title card when you know the name of the book but not who wrote it. You use the subject card if you do not have any authors or titles in mind but are looking for a book on a particular topic. The call number tells you where to find the book on the library shelf.

▶ Use Your Research

New information gathered from your research can be added to your story map. This writer found some flower names and other information during her research. How did she change her map?

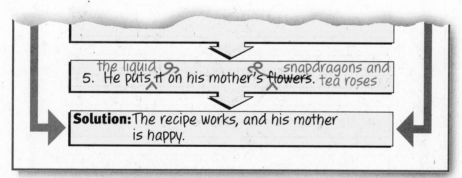

PRACTICE AND APPLY

Review Your Plan

1. Look at your story map.

2. List questions you have about events in your story.

3. Look in the card catalog in the library or media center to identify the resources you will need to find answers.

4. Add new information you gather to your story map.

PREWRITE

DRAFT

REVISE

PROOFREAD

PUBLISH

Checklist ✓

Research and Inquiry

- **Did you list your questions on index cards?**

- **Did you identify possible resources?**

- **Did you take notes or print out helpful information?**

Draft

Before you begin writing your story, review the story map you made. Identify the beginning, middle, and end of your story. Consider making a paragraph for each. Also, think about the characters' dialogue. You will need to put each new speaker's words in a separate paragraph.

Beginning: Introduces characters, setting, and problem

✓ Checklist

Drafting

- Is your story well suited to your purpose and audience?

- Have you introduced the characters, setting, and problem of the plot?

- Are the events in your story arranged in a logical order?

- Did you include dialogue that sounds like something the characters would say?

- Does the ending of your story solve the problem in the plot?

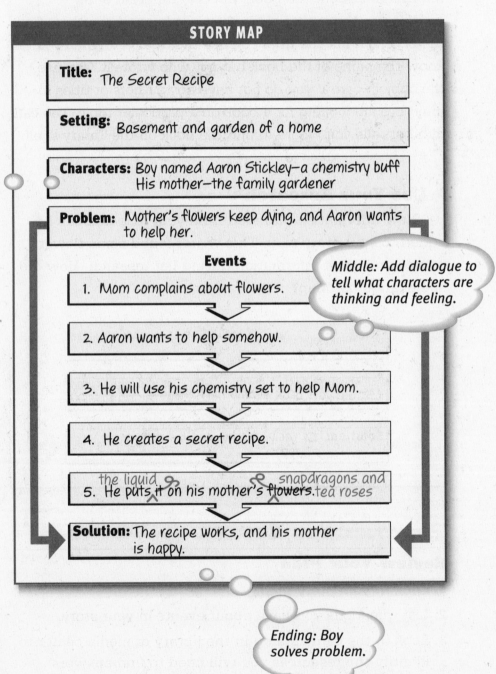

STORY MAP

Title: The Secret Recipe

Setting: Basement and garden of a home

Characters: Boy named Aaron Stickley—a chemistry buff
His mother—the family gardener

Problem: Mother's flowers keep dying, and Aaron wants to help her.

Events

1. Mom complains about flowers.

2. Aaron wants to help somehow.

3. He will use his chemistry set to help Mom.

4. He creates a secret recipe.

5. He puts ~~it~~ the liquid on his mother's ~~flowers~~ snapdragons and tea roses.

Solution: The recipe works, and his mother is happy.

Middle: Add dialogue to tell what characters are thinking and feeling.

Ending: Boy solves problem.

Notice how this writer used the ideas in her story map to write a first draft. She began by introducing the characters and setting in her first paragraph. The writer also used dialogue to express the characters' thoughts and feelings.

PREWRITE

DRAFT

REVISE

PROOFREAD

PUBLISH

DRAFT

The Secret Recipe

Aaron Stickley was experimenting. Suddenly, he heard his mother groan from their backyard.

"What's the matter, Mom." Aaron asked. "My flowers won't grow" Aaron's Mother said.

That's all Aaron needed to hear. Soon he had made a concoction. he knew this would solve his mother's problem.

Aaron's mother looked doubtful, but she fed the flowers with the liquid, anyway.

Aaron and his mother checked the flowers the snapdragons were blooming and tea roses covered the fence. "You're amazing," his mother exclaimed.

Aaron smiled and thought, "Gee thanks, Mom. Just wait until you need help growing tomatoes!"

First paragraph introduces characters and setting.

Dialogue helps state the problem and makes the characters and events come to life.

Gives a possible solution to the problem in the story

Strong, funny ending

PRACTICE AND APPLY

Draft Your Own Story

1. Review your story map.

2. Introduce characters, setting, and a problem.

3. Give events in the order they happened.

4. Use dialogue to describe characters.

TiP!

TECHNOLOGY

Give your document a name that you will remember. You may wish to include the word *draft* in the name.

Revise

Elaborate

One way to improve your writing is to elaborate. When you elaborate, you add important ideas and details that will make your writing clearer and more interesting. When you revise your story, you may need to add more vivid and descriptive language.

The details that the writer added lets the reader "see" the setting, characters, and events in the story.

> conducting chemistry experiments in the basement
> Aaron Stickley was experimenting. ^

The writer added the fact that Aaron and his mother checked the flowers the next morning to help readers follow the sequence of events in the story.

> The next morning,
> ^Aaron and his mother checked the flowers

Word Choice

When you are writing, it is important to choose just the right words for your topic and audience. Vivid verbs and vivid adjectives help give exact meaning and also make a story come alive..

> replied
> "My flowers won't grow" Aaron's Mother said. ^
> stirred up
> That's all Aaron needed to hear. Soon he had made
> bubbling   "This is your answer, Mom," Aaron announced.
> a concoction. he knew this would solve his mother's
> problem.

DIALOGUE WORDS

said
replied
asked
cried
announced
answered
remarked
exclaimed
suggested
responded
stated
whispered

Better Paragraphs

As you continue to revise your draft, check to be sure that you have used a new paragraph each time the speaker changes. Also check to see that each paragraph without dialogue contains a group of related ideas. By indenting your paragraphs, you are signaling to your reader that here is a "chunk" of related material.

> Aaron's mother looked doubtful, but she fed the
> flowers with the ^syripy liquid, anyway.
> ^The next morning, Aaron and his mother checked the flowers the
> snapdragons were blooming and tea roses ^wildly covered
> the fence.

PRACTICE AND APPLY

Revise Your Own Story

1. Add dialogue to bring your characters to life and to make your story more interesting.

2. Group related thoughts into paragraphs.

3. **Grammar** Did you begin a quotation with a capital letter and use quotation marks around a speaker's words?

TECHNOLOGY

Do you sometimes forget to indent paragraphs? Many word-processing programs allow you to set margins so that the first line of a paragraph indents automatically.

Revise • Peer Conferencing

Get a different view of your writing. Exchange drafts with a partner. Someone else may have some fresh ideas or suggestions that you haven't thought of yourself.

I think your title could be better.

Good beginning—include more details about the character.

Can you describe this in more vivid detail?

I like this ending. It's funny!

> The Secret Recipe
>
> Aaron Stickley was experimenting. Suddenly, he heard his mother groan from their backyard.
>
> "What's the matter, Mom." Aaron asked.
>
> "My flowers won't grow." Aaron's Mother said.
>
> That's all Aaron needed to hear. Soon he had made a concoction. he knew this would solve his mother's problem.
>
> Aaron's mother looked doubtful, but she fed the flowers with the liquid, anyway.
>
> Aaron and his mother checked the flowers the snapdragons were blooming and tea roses covered the fence. "You're amazing," his mother exclaimed.
>
> Aaron smiled and thought, "Gee thanks, Mom. Just wait until you need help growing tomatoes!"

Conferencing for the Reader

- Are features of a story included in your partner's draft?
  - strong beginning, middle, and end
  - interesting characters, setting, and plot
  - problem that's solved at the end
  - descriptive words
  - dialogue
  - strong ending
- Make sure to tell your partner what you like about his or her work, as well as what you think needs improvement.

Writing PROCESS

Before you revise your story, think about the comments and suggestions your conferencing partner gave you. This writer made some changes based on her partner's ideas.

PREWRITE

DRAFT

REVISE

PROOFREAD

PUBLISH

REVISE

A Growing Problem
~~The Secret Recipe~~

Brainy   conducting chemistry experiments in the basement
Aaron Stickley was ~~experimenting~~. Suddenly, he

heard his mother groan from their backyard.

"What's the matter, Mom." Aaron asked. "My

replied
flowers won't grow" Aaron's Mother ~~said~~.

That's all Aaron needed to hear. Soon he had
stirred up bubbling "This is your answer, Mom,"
made a concoction. ~~he knew this would solve his~~
Aaron announced.
~~mother's problem.~~

Aaron's mother looked doubtful, but she fed the
syripy
flowers with the liquid, anyway.
The next morning,
Aaron and his mother checked the flowers the
a sea of pink waves the massive wildly
snapdragons were ~~blooming~~ and tea roses ~~covered the~~
clung to the fence for dear life
~~fence~~. "You're amazing," his mother exclaimed.

Aaron smiled and thought, "Gee thanks, Mom.

Just wait until you need help growing tomatoes!"

PRACTICE AND APPLY

Revise Your Own Story

1. Read your draft aloud, or have your partner read it to you. Listen for the rhythm and flow of your sentences.

2. Use the notes from your peer conference to help improve your draft.

3. Replace plain words with more vivid language.

4. Add a title that will "grab" your audience's interest.

Checklist ✓

Revising

- Will your story entertain your audience?

- Do you need to elaborate on any part of your story to make your ideas clearer?

- Did you choose words that describe?

- Did you write the events in the correct order?

- Do your sentences flow together naturally?

- Did you add an interesting title?

Proofread/Edit

After you have revised your story, you will need to proofread and edit it to find and correct any mistakes in mechanics, grammar and usage, and spelling.

STRATEGIES FOR PROOFREADING

- **Reread your revised paper.** Look for a different type of error each time you read.

- **Read each sentence and paragraph for correct capitalization and punctuation.** Pay special attention to where dialogue appears.

- **Check that you have indented your paragraphs.** Make sure you have indented to show when a different character is speaking.

- **Check for spelling mistakes.** Use a dictionary or a spell checker to check for errors.

TECHNOLOGY

Remember that a spell checker cannot catch misused words that are spelled correctly. If you type *the* instead of *they*, the mistake will not be caught. Also, a spell checker may not catch misspelled names.

REVIEW THE RULES

GRAMMAR

- The tense of a verb tells whether the action takes place in the present, past, or future. An irregular verb is a verb that does not add *-ed* to form the past tense. The spelling of the verb changes to form the past tense.

MECHANICS

- Capitalize the first word of a direct quotation. A direct quotation gives a speaker's exact words.

- Use a comma to set off a direct quotation from words such as *he said* or *she said*.

- Use quotation marks before and after a direct quotation.

- Place a period or a comma inside closing quotation marks.

- Place a question mark or an exclamation mark inside the quotation marks when it is part of the entire sentence.

Go to pages 138–169 to review other rules.

Look at the proofreading corrections made on the draft below. What does the symbol ≡ mean? Why does the writer want to start a new sentence?

PROOFREAD

A Growing Problem
~~The Secret Recipe~~

Brainy conducting chemistry experiments in the basement
Aaron Stickley was ~~experimenting~~. Suddenly, he

heard his mother groan from their backyard.

?
"What's the matter, Mom." Aaron asked. # "My

replied
flowers won't grow." Aaron's Mother said.

That's all Aaron needed to hear. Soon he had

stirred up bubbling "This is your answer, Mom,"
made a concoction. ~~he knew this would solve his~~

Aaron announced.
~~mother's problem.~~

Aaron's mother looked doubtful, but she fed the

~~syripy~~ SP syrupy
flowers with the liquid, anyway.

The next morning,
Aaron and his mother checked the flowers the

a sea of pink waves, the massive wildly
snapdragons were ~~blooming and~~ tea roses ~~covered the~~

clung to the fence for dear life
~~fence~~. "You're amazing," his mother exclaimed.

Aaron smiled and thought, "Gee, thanks, Mom.

Just wait until you need help growing tomatoes!"

Checklist ✔

Proofreading

- Did you spell all your words correctly?

- Did you begin and end dialogue with quotation marks?

- Did you capitalize the first word of a direct quotation and end with the correct punctuation mark?

- Did you indent each paragraph?

PROOFREADING MARKS

#	new paragraph
∧	add
ℛ	take out
≡	Make a capital letter.
/	Make a small letter.
SP	Check the spelling.
⊙	Add a period.

PRACTICE AND APPLY

Proofread Your Own Story

1. Correct any spelling errors.

2. Include correct capitalization and punctuation for dialogue.

3. Use the Proofreading Checklist.

Publish

Before you publish your story, review your writing one last time. A checklist can help you focus on your work.

✔ Self-Check Fictional Narrative

☐ Who was my audience? Did I write in a way that will interest them?

☐ What was my purpose in telling this story? Will my audience be entertained?

☐ Did I begin and end my story in an interesting way?

☐ Did I include enough details so that my audience can "see" my characters, setting, and events?

☐ Did I make my sequence of events clear?

☐ Does my ending include the solution to the problem?

☐ Did I use long and short sentences to make my writing more interesting?

☐ Did I proofread and correct all errors?

The writer used the checklist to review her story. Read "A Growing Problem" and discuss the writer's published work. Do you think it was ready to publish? Why do you think so?

A Growing Problem

by Dara MacKenzie

Brainy Aaron Stickley was conducting chemistry experiments in the basement. Suddenly, he heard his mother groan from their backyard.

"What's the matter, Mom?" Aaron asked.

"My flowers won't grow," Aaron's mother replied.

That's all Aaron needed to hear. Soon he had stirred up a bubbling concoction. "This is your answer, Mom," Aaron announced.

Aaron's mother looked doubtful, but she fed the flowers with the syrupy liquid, anyway.

The next morning, Aaron and his mother checked the flowers. The snapdragons were a sea of pink waves, and the massive tea roses wildly clung to the fence for dear life. "You're amazing," his mother exclaimed.

Aaron smiled and thought, "Gee, thanks, Mom. Just wait until you need help growing tomatoes!"

TECHNOLOGY

Experiment with different font styles. Use a font that goes with the humorous mood of your story, but be sure it is easy to read.

PRACTICE AND APPLY

Publish Your Own Story

1. Check your draft one last time.

2. Make a neat, final copy.

3. Make sure the title and your name are easy to read.

4. Add a border, pictures, or a cover.

Fictional Narrative: A Story

Score	Description
4 Excellent	- creates an entertaining, imaginative story - moves readers through an engaging beginning, middle, and end - uses a clear and believable voice and unique narrative style - uses rich, precise language, including figurative language - includes a variety of sentences that have rhythm and flow - is free or almost free of errors
3 Good	- creates an imaginative, interesting story - has a well-planned plot with a clear beginning, middle, and end - uses an original voice that is consistent with plot and characters - uses clear and concise language with both new and everyday words - includes both simple and compound sentences - has minor errors that do not confuse the reader
2 Fair	- creates a fairly imaginative story with some details about character and plot - has a confusing narrative - attempts a narrative voice but does not engage or entertain the reader - uses ordinary words that sometimes repeat - lacks sentence variety - makes frequent errors that confuse the reader
1 Unsatisfactory	- creates a story lacking in imagination - presents story details in a confusing, illogical manner - does not use a distinct narrative voice - uses words that are either incorrect or unrelated to the story - contains confusing run-on sentences and sentence fragments - makes serious and repeated errors

Go to www.macmillanmh.com for a 6-Point Student Writing Rubric.

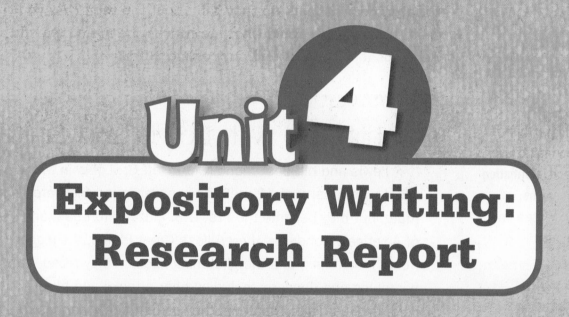

Unit 4
Expository Writing: Research Report

Expository Writing

Have you ever written interesting facts about a person, place, or thing? Your factual account was an example of expository writing. Expository writing presents readers with important research and information about a topic.

Learning from Writers

Read the following examples of expository writing. What important facts do they tell about the topic? As you read, notice how each author introduces the main idea and develops it with facts and supporting details.

THINK AND WRITE

Purpose
Why do you think it is important to give facts and information in a magazine article? Write a brief explanation.

Catching Up with Lewis and Clark

Lewis and his best friend, Clark, left St. Louis in May 1804 with a party of 42 men. They never found the water route, but they became the first U.S. citizens to see many of America's wonders—the endless Great Plains, the jagged Rocky Mountains, and the glistening Pacific. They faced many hardships and dangers, including bear attacks and bitter cold. In Great Falls, Montana, they carried heavy canoes for weeks around waterfalls under the hot sun. At times they had little food to eat and almost starved.

More than 500 days and 4,000 miles after they had set out, Lewis and Clark reached the Pacific. "Ocían in view! O! the joy!" wrote Clark in his journal. (Clark was smart and brave, but not a very good speller.)

The explorers kept superb maps and diaries. They were the first to describe 122 kinds of animals and 176 plants, and to meet many native tribes. But they left barely a trace behind at their campsites. That makes it hard for historians to say "Lewis and Clark were here!"

—from "Catching Up with Lewis and Clark," in *Time for Kids*

The Lewis and Clark Expedition

Traveling across a land with no roads and no maps, two young men explored a vast unknown territory. After two and a half years, the young adventurers returned from their eight-thousand-mile journey. Lewis and Clark had tales to tell.

Thomas Jefferson chose Lewis and Clark to lead an expedition of 42 men to explore the land west of the Mississippi. The group left St. Louis in May 1804.

The explorers struggled hard; however, in November 1805 they reached the Pacific Ocean. After spending the winter there, they began their return trip.

The members of the expedition had been given up for lost, but they arrived back at St. Louis in September 1806. They brought with them glowing reports of the land and the Native American groups who had helped them on their journey.   —Teresa Jiménez

PRACTICE AND APPLY

Thinking Like a Reader

1. What is the main idea of each paragraph in "Catching Up with Lewis and Clark"?

2. What is the most important information in "The Lewis and Clark Expedition"?

Thinking Like a Writer

3. How did the author of "Catching Up with Lewis and Clark" support his main ideas?

4. How did the author of "The Lewis and Clark Expedition" summarize her information in the conclusion?

5. **Reading Across Texts** Compare the introductions and the conclusions of the two literature models. How are they alike and different?

Features of Expository Writing

GUIDELINES

Expository writing gives facts and information about a topic. Good expository writing:

▶ introduces the **main idea** and develops it with facts and **supporting details.**

▶ gives **important information** about a specific topic.

▶ summarizes research from **a variety of sources.**

▶ uses **transition words** to connect ideas.

▶ draws a **conclusion** based on the facts and information presented.

▶ Main Idea and Supporting Details

Reread "Catching Up with Lewis and Clark" on page 68. What is the main idea of the article? What facts and supporting details tell about the main idea?

> Lewis and his best friend, Clark, left St. Louis in May 1804 with a party of 42 men.

This sentence from the first paragraph tells you the main focus of the selection. The facts and details in the rest of the selection help explain what happens to the explorers after they leave St. Louis.

▶ Important Information

You can use expository writing to share important information with your audience. What important information does the author share in this sentence?

> They were the first to describe 122 kinds of animals and 176 plants, and to meet many native tribes.

This sentence gives you specific information about the discoveries that Lewis and Clark made during their journey.

▶ A Variety of Sources

To present the most accurate and complete information about your topic, it is important to summarize facts and details from a variety of sources. Where might the author have researched this information?

> "Ocían in view! O! the joy!" wrote Clark in his journal.

The author could have used encyclopedias, books, documentaries, and Clark's own journal to gather information.

▶ Transition Words

To help your readers clearly understand important information, you need to use transition words that connect the events and ideas in your writing. Words such as *at times, after,* and *however* help you connect ideas.

> More than 500 days and 4,000 miles after they had set out, Lewis and Clark reached the Pacific.

What transition word did the author use?

▶ A Conclusion

The author ends "Catching Up with Lewis and Clark" by drawing a conclusion.

> That makes it hard for historians to say "Lewis and Clark were here!"

On what information does the author base this conclusion?

PRACTICE AND APPLY

Create a Main Idea and Supporting Details Chart

1. Reread "The Lewis and Clark Expedition" by Teresa Jiménez on page 69.

2. Create a Main Idea and Supporting Details chart.

3. Write the main idea of the piece at the bottom of the chart. Then list the supporting details.

4. What kinds of sources do you think Teresa used to find her information?

Details

Main Idea

Prewrite

Expository writing presents facts about a particular topic. You can use expository writing to share important information with your readers. Often, this information is in the form of a research report.

Purpose and Audience

The purpose of expository writing is to give your readers information. In this way, expository writing lets you share important facts and ideas with your audience.

Before you begin to write, think about your audience. How will you present your ideas? Once you have chosen your topic, consider what your audience already knows about it. This will help you decide the kind of information to include in your report.

Choose a Topic

Start by **brainstorming** a list of topics. Focus on topics you have read or heard about in school or at home, or have seen on a television news program. Consider both past and current events. Then choose a topic.

Once you have chosen your topic, **explore ideas**. Make a list of facts. Later, you will organize these facts in an outline.

Audience
What kind of information will you give an audience who knows something about your topic? Write your ideas in your journal.

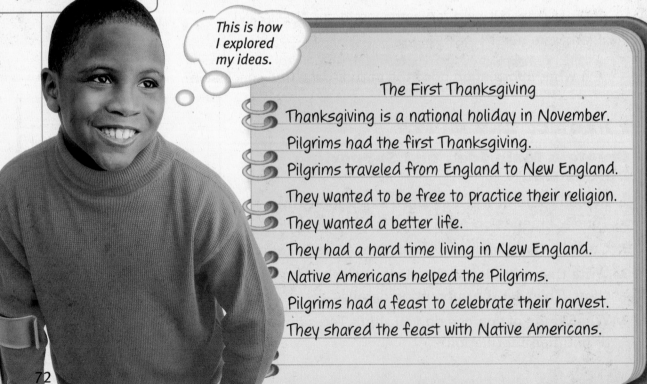

This is how I explored my ideas.

The First Thanksgiving

Thanksgiving is a national holiday in November.

Pilgrims had the first Thanksgiving.

Pilgrims traveled from England to New England.

They wanted to be free to practice their religion.

They wanted a better life.

They had a hard time living in New England.

Native Americans helped the Pilgrims.

Pilgrims had a feast to celebrate their harvest.

They shared the feast with Native Americans.

Organize • Outlining

The facts and details in expository writing are organized around an introduction, a body, and a conclusion. The introduction tells the main idea of the topic. The body develops the topic, and the conclusion summarizes the information. Notice that the writer does not include all the items on his list.

PREWRITE

DRAFT

REVISE

PROOFREAD

PUBLISH

OUTLINE

The First Thanksgiving

I. Introduction
    A. Pilgrims had the first Thanksgiving.
II. Moving to New England
    A. Pilgrims traveled from England to New England.
        1. Settled Plymouth Colony

    B. They wanted a better life.

III. Life in New England
    A. Pilgrims had a hard time living in New England.
        1. Not enough food

    B. Native Americans helped the Pilgrims

IV. Conclusion
    A. Pilgrims had a feast to celebrate their harvest.

    B. They shared the feast with Native Americans.

Checklist ✓
Prewriting

- Did you think about your purpose and audience?

- Did you choose a topic that will interest your readers?

- Did you identify the main points you want to present?

- Did you group together similar facts and details?

- Did you organize your ideas in an outline?

- What kind of research do you need to do to gather important information?

PRACTICE AND APPLY

Plan Your Expository Writing

1. Think about your purpose and audience.
2. Brainstorm a list of possible topics.
3. Choose a topic and explore ideas.
4. Use an outline to organize facts and ideas.

Prewrite • Research and Inquiry

▶ Writer's Resources

To get more information for your report, you will have to do research. First, write questions to guide you. Then decide which resources you will need to answer them.

What Else Do I Need to Know?	Where Can I Find the Information?
When did the first Thanksgiving take place?	Read a historical time line.
Why did the Pilgrims start a new colony?	Watch documentaries and videos about the topic.

▶ Use a Time Line

You can discover when an event took place by looking at a time line. A time line is a diagram that shows when a series of events took place. Time lines help you keep track of the order of events.

The time line below shows some of the important events that led to the Pilgrims' decision to start the Plymouth Colony. It also shows the events that led to the celebration of the first Thanksgiving.

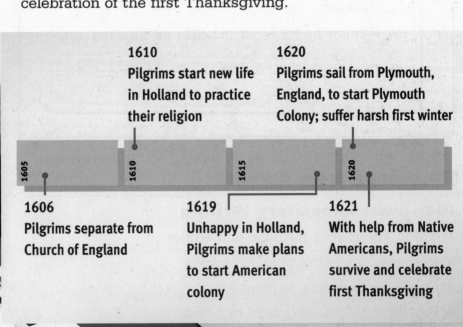

1610
Pilgrims start new life in Holland to practice their religion

1620
Pilgrims sail from Plymouth, England, to start Plymouth Colony; suffer harsh first winter

1605 — 1610 — 1615 — 1620

1606
Pilgrims separate from Church of England

1619
Unhappy in Holland, Pilgrims make plans to start American colony

1621
With help from Native Americans, Pilgrims survive and celebrate first Thanksgiving

Writing PROCESS

► View Documentaries and Videos

Documentaries and videos can be helpful sources of information. These visuals can provide important facts and interesting details to include in your writing. Be sure to take notes or draw quick sketches of what you see.

► Use Your Research

After completing your research, add any new facts to your outline. This writer learned important information from the time line. He also learned about the Pilgrims' first year in New England by looking at historical videos and documentaries.

I. Introduction

  A. Pilgrims had the first Thanksgiving. *in 1621*

II. Moving to New England

  A. Pilgrims traveled from England to New England.

    1. Settled Plymouth Colony

    2. Landed in 1620

  B. They wanted a better life.

    1. Freedom to practice their religion

III. Life in New England

  A. Pilgrims had a hard time living in New England.

    1. Not enough food

    2. Many Pilgrims died.

  B. Native Americans helped the Pilgrims

    1. Met Squanto in March 1621

    2. He taught Pilgrims to fish and plant crops.

Checklist ✓

Research and Inquiry

■ Did you list questions about your topic?

■ Did you identify possible resources?

■ Did you take notes about the facts you read?

PRACTICE AND APPLY

Review Your Plan

1. Look at your outline.

2. List questions you have about your topic.

3. Identify the resources you will need.

4. Gather facts from a variety of sources.

5. Add new facts to your outline.

Draft

Writing PROCESS

Before you begin writing your report, review the outline you have made. Plan to make a paragraph for each idea that is indicated by a Roman numeral. The facts marked with capital letters and the details indicated by numbers should support the main idea of each paragraph.

Main idea for report: Pilgrims had the first Thanksgiving

Main idea for second paragraph: Moving to New England

Main idea for third paragraph: Life in New England

✓ Checklist

Drafting

- Remember your purpose and audience.

- Give important information about a specific topic.

- Be sure that your facts and details in each paragraph support the main idea.

- Write a strong introduction, body, and conclusion.

- Draw a conclusion based on the facts and details you presented.

OUTLINE

The First Thanksgiving

I. Introduction   in 1621

   A. Pilgrims had the first Thanksgiving.

II. Moving to New England

   A. Pilgrims traveled from England to New England.

      1. Settled Plymouth Colony
      2. Landed in 1620

   B. They wanted a better life.
      1. Freedom to practice their religion

III. Life in New England

   A. Pilgrims had a hard time living in New England.

      1. Not enough food
      2. Many Pilgrims died.

   B. Native Americans helped the Pilgrims
      1. Met Squanto in March 1621
      2. He taught Pilgrims to fish and plant crops.

IV. Conclusion

   A. Pilgrims had a feast to celebrate their harvest.
      1. Three-day feast

   B. They shared the feast with Native Americans.

The last paragraph will be my conclusion.

This writer used the ideas in his outline to write a first draft. He stated the main idea of his report in a topic sentence. The writer added details about Squanto and the Pilgrims. He referred to a video to show the source of his facts.

PREWRITE

DRAFT

REVISE

PROOFREAD

PUBLISH

DRAFT

Many experts beleive that the first Thanksgiving took place in the Plymouth colony in 1621.

In the video Journey to Freedom, Robert Nang explains how the Pilgrims made the long journey to New England in 1620. It was a hard journey.

Mr Nang shows that the Pilgrims worked hard in the Plymouth colony to make a new life. Unfortunately, with little food or help, many Pilgrims died. In March of 1621, help arrived. A Native american man named Squanto taught the Pilgrims how to fish. He taught them how to plant corn and other new crops. With Squantos help, the fall brought a great harvest

The Pilgrims were thankful for the harvest. They held a three-day feast. They invited some Native Americans to help them celebrate.

Topic sentence of report

Includes facts from a reliable source

Main idea of paragraph: Life in New England

Supporting details tell how Squanto helped the Pilgrims to survive.

PRACTICE AND APPLY

Draft Your Expository Writing

1. Review your prewriting outline.
2. State the main idea of the report in a topic sentence.
3. Write events in the order in which they happened.
4. Use facts and details to support your main ideas.

TECHNOLOGY

If you typed the outline on the computer during prewriting, use the same document to begin your writing. Be sure each item in the outline is a full sentence in your draft.

Revise

Elaborate

One way to improve your writing is to elaborate. When you elaborate, you add important ideas, facts, and details that might be missing from your writing. When you revise your expository writing, you may need to tell more information about key events.

The information that this writer added lets the reader know when an event happened.

> Unfortunately, with little food or help, many Pilgrims
> that first winter
> died.
> ^

The writer added a fact to make clear which Native Americans were invited to the celebration.

> Squanto and some of his friends
> They invited ~~some Native Americans~~ to help them celebrate.
> ^

Word Choice

When you are writing an expository piece such as a research report, it is important to choose the right words for your topic and audience.

In expository writing, you need to find words that will help you order your information and connect your ideas. These words are called *transition words*.

> In March of 1621, help arrived. A Native american man
> named Squanto taught the Pilgrims how to fish. He
> taught them how to plant corn and other new crops.
> In fact,
> With Squantos help, the fall brought a great harvest
> ^

TRANSITION WORDS

however
yet
in fact
for example
as a result
because
therefore
so that
fortunately
now
then
finally

Better Paragraphs

As you revise your draft, check your paragraphs to make sure they fit together well. Read the paragraphs aloud. Do the details in each paragraph support the main idea? Does the information flow from one paragraph to the next? Rearranging paragraphs or changing parts of a paragraph may improve the overall flow of your report.

You can add, take out, move information, or add transitions to connect the ideas in one or more paragraphs.

> In the video <u>Journey to Freedom</u>, Robert Nang explains how the Pilgrims made the long journey to New England in 1620. It was a hard journey.
>
> Mr Nang shows that the Pilgrims worked hard in the Plymouth colony to make a new life. Unfortunately, that first winter with little food or help, many Pilgrims died. In March of 1621, help arrived.

TECHNOLOGY

Review your draft for logical order. Do the ideas flow smoothly? If not, try moving paragraphs or sentences around by cutting and pasting text.

PRACTICE AND APPLY

Revise Your Expository Writing

1. Add facts and details that will support the main idea of each paragraph and give more information to the reader.

2. Use transition words to connect ideas.

3. Change or rearrange information so that ideas "build up" from beginning to end.

4. **Grammar** Should you replace any nouns with the appropriate pronouns?

Revise • Peer Conferencing

Take a break from your writing. Exchange first drafts with a partner. Listen to all your partner's suggestions. Take notes. Make those changes with which you agree.

Writing PROCESS

Many experts beleive that the first Thanksgiving took place in the Plymouth colony in 1621.

In the video <u>Journey to Freedom</u>, Robert Nang explains how the Pilgrims made the long journey to New England in 1620. It was a hard journey.

Mr Nang shows that the Pilgrims worked hard in the Plymouth colony to make a new life. Unfortunately, with little food or help, many Pilgrims died. In March of 1621, help arrived. A Native american man named Squanto taught the Pilgrims how to fish. He taught them how to plant corn and other new crops. With Squantos help, the fall brought a great harvest

The Pilgrims were thankful for the harvest. They held a three-day feast. They invited some Native Americans to help them celebrate.

Combine the adjectives in these two sentences.

You should add why the Pilgrims came to New England.

You should combine these two sentences into one.

Say that this was the first Thanksgiving.

Conferencing for the Reader

- Are features of expository writing included in your partner's piece?
  - introduces a main idea and details
  - summarizes information from different sources
  - draws a conclusion
  - uses transitions
- Discuss with your partner things that you like about his or her writing as well as things that you think need revising.

Think about the comments and suggestions your conferencing partner gave you. Use the ideas to revise your report. This writer made some changes based on his partner's ideas.

PREWRITE

DRAFT

REVISE

PROOFREAD

PUBLISH

REVISE

How Thanksgiving Came to Be

Many experts beleive that the first Thanksgiving took place in the Plymouth colony in 1621.

In the video Journey to Freedom, Robert Nang explains how the Pilgrims made the long hard journey to New England in 1620. ~~It was a hard journey.~~

Mr Nang shows that the Pilgrims worked hard in the Plymouth colony to practice their religion and make a new life. Unfortunately, that first winter with little food or help, many Pilgrims died. In March of 1621, help arrived. A Native american man named Squanto taught the Pilgrims how to fish, and ~~He taught them how to~~ plant corn and other new crops. In fact, With Squantos help, the fall brought a great harvest and ~~The Pilgrims were thankful for the harvest.~~ They held a three-day feast. They invited Squanto and some of his friends ~~some Native Americans~~ to help them celebrate. That feast was probably the first Thanksgiving.

PRACTICE AND APPLY

Revise Your Expository Writing

1. Read the notes from your peer conference.

2. Use your partner's suggestions to improve your draft.

3. Take out any unimportant facts or details.

4. If you need to add important facts, do more research.

Checklist ✓

Revising

- Does your report suit your purpose and audience?

- Does your topic sentence clearly state the main idea of your report?

- Do you need to elaborate on any part of your report?

- Did you write the events in the right order?

- Did you check your facts in more than one source?

- Do your sentences and paragraphs flow smoothly?

- Did you write a title that explains the topic?

Proofread/Edit

After you have revised your expository writing, you will need to proofread and edit it to find and correct any mistakes in mechanics, grammar and usage, and spelling.

STRATEGIES FOR PROOFREADING

- **Read your revised report more than once.** Look for a different kind of error each time. You'll have a better chance of catching all errors.

- **Check each sentence for correct capitalization.** Remember to capitalize proper nouns and proper adjectives.

- **Reread for correct punctuation.** These include commas, apostrophes, and end marks.

- **Check for spelling mistakes by reading your paper backward, from the last word to the first.** This will help you focus on the spelling of each word.

TECHNOLOGY

It is often easier to catch mistakes on paper than on a computer screen. For proofreading, print out your work, mark the corrections on paper, and then enter the corrections to the file.

REVIEW THE RULES

GRAMMAR

- An **adjective** is a word that describes a noun or a pronoun and tells *what kind, which one,* or *how many.* You can use an adjective to combine two sentences that tell about the same noun or pronoun. When you combine two sentences, leave out words that repeat.

- A **pronoun** takes the place of one or more nouns. Pronouns can be singular or plural and can be used as either subjects or objects in a sentence.

MECHANICS

- An **abbreviation** is a shortened form of a word. Most abbreviations begin with a **capital letter** and end with a **period.**

Go to pages 138–169 to review other rules.

Look at the proofreading corrections made on the draft below. What does the symbol / mean? Why does the writer need to use a small letter?

PREWRITE

DRAFT

REVISE

PROOFREAD

PUBLISH

PROOFREAD

How Thanksgiving Came to Be

(SP) believe
¶ Many experts ~~beleive~~ that the first Thanksgiving

took place in the Plymouth colony in 1621.

In the video Journey to Freedom, Robert Nang

, hard
explains how the Pilgrims made the long journey to

New England in 1620. ~~It was a hard journey.~~

Mr. Nang shows that the Pilgrims worked hard in
practice their religion and
the Plymouth colony to make a new life. Unfortunately,
that first winter
with little food or help, many Pilgrims died. In March

of 1621, help arrived. A Native american man named

and
Squanto taught the Pilgrims how to fish. He taught

In fact,
~~them how to plant corn~~ and other new crops. With

Squanto's help, the fall brought a great harvest.

, and
The Pilgrims were thankful for the harvest. They

Squanto and some of his friends
held a three-day feast. They invited ~~some Native~~
That feast was probably the first Thanksgiving.
~~Americans~~ to help them celebrate.

Checklist ✓

Proofreading

- Did you spell all the words correctly?

- Did you use correct punctuation?

- Did you capitalize proper nouns, proper adjectives, titles, and the beginning of every sentence?

- Did you indent each paragraph?

PROOFREADING MARKS

¶	new paragraph
∧	add
ꝰ	take out
≡	Make a capital letter.
/	Make a small letter.
SP	Check the spelling.
⊙	Add a period.

PRACTICE AND APPLY

Proofread Your Expository Writing

1. Correct spelling mistakes.

2. Check for correct use of commas, apostrophes, and other punctuation marks.

3. Be sure that proper nouns and proper adjectives begin with a capital letter.

4. Indent paragraphs.

Publish

Before you publish your report, check your writing one last time. You can use a checklist to help you focus on the review of your work.

✓ Self-Check   Expository Writing

- ❑ Who was my audience? Did I give them enough information about my topic?

- ❑ What was my main topic? Did I include enough facts and details to support it?

- ❑ Did I begin in a clear and interesting way? Did I summarize my ideas at the end?

- ❑ Did I present my information in the best order? Did I use the right transition words to connect my ideas?

- ❑ Did I combine sentences? Do my sentences flow together?

- ❑ Are my paragraphs fully developed with important information? Do I have a clear introduction, body, and conclusion?

- ❑ Did I proofread and correct all errors?

The writer used the checklist to review his report. Read "How Thanksgiving Came to Be" and discuss the writer's published piece. Jot down your thoughts about the report. Did the writer include enough information? Do you think the report was ready to be published? What else would you like to know about the topic?

Writing PROCESS

How Thanksgiving Came to Be

by Jamal Travers

Many experts believe that the first Thanksgiving took place in the Plymouth Colony in 1621.

In the video *Journey to Freedom*, Robert Nang explains how the Pilgrims made the long, hard journey to New England in 1620. Mr. Nang shows that the Pilgrims worked hard in the Plymouth Colony to practice their religion and make a new life.

Unfortunately, with little food or help, many Pilgrims died that first winter. In March of 1621, help arrived. A Native American man named Squanto taught the Pilgrims how to fish and plant corn and other new crops. In fact, with Squanto's help, the fall brought a great harvest.

The Pilgrims were thankful for the harvest, and they held a three-day feast. They invited Squanto and some of his friends to help them celebrate. That feast was probably the first Thanksgiving.

PRACTICE AND APPLY

Publish Your Expository Writing

1. Check your revised draft one more time.
2. Write or print out a neat, final copy of your draft.
3. Add pictures, a Thanksgiving border, or a cover.

TECHNOLOGY

There are many fonts and borders you can use to make your published piece clearer and more attractive. Experiment with different styles and sizes before making your final decision.

Research Report

Score	Description
4 **Excellent**	▪ uses reliable sources and has interesting, unusual facts ▪ is well structured and has a strong introduction and conclusion ▪ shows awareness of readers and a sense of purpose throughout ▪ uses transition words and a vivid vocabulary ▪ uses sentences that flow smoothly and hold the reader's interest ▪ is free or almost free of errors
3 **Good**	▪ uses reliable sources and has a main idea and supporting details ▪ has a logical flow of facts and details ▪ shows a good awareness of readers and a sense of purpose ▪ uses relevant language and transition words ▪ uses a variety of simple and complex sentences ▪ has minor errors that do not confuse the reader
2 **Fair**	▪ presents a report with some facts based on limited research ▪ has sections that are hard to follow ▪ does not show awareness of readers and shows little understanding of topic ▪ chooses weak words for topic with few transition words ▪ uses awkward phrasing and choppy sentences ▪ makes frequent errors that confuse the reader
1 **Unsatisfactory**	▪ presents a report that is not researched with either no or inaccurate facts ▪ is structured poorly and is impossible to follow ▪ does not address readers and shows little or no understanding of topic ▪ relies on basic vocabulary with no transition words ▪ includes incomplete and run-on sentences ▪ makes serious and repeated errors

Go to www.macmillanmh.com for a 6-Point Student Writing Rubric.

Unit 5
Expository Writing: Writing That Compares

Writing That Compares

Have you ever compared two people or things? Then you probably have noticed that the two items were alike in some ways and different in others. In writing that compares, you often do the same thing. This type of writing gives you the chance to describe how two items are alike yet also different.

Learning from Writers

Read these examples of descriptive writing. What are the writers comparing? Why do you think they used this form of writing to explain their topic?

THiNK AND WRITE

Purpose
What reasons might a writer have for comparing two people, things, or ideas? Write your thoughts in your journal.

Is a Doctor Like a Merchant?

For example, suppose I were to see two people coming toward me. Let us say that one is a Merchant (an Equilateral Triangle) and the other is a Doctor (a Pentagon). Both appear to be Straight Lines, so how am I to tell one from the other?

In the case of the Merchant, I see a Straight Line, of course. The center of this line, which is the part nearest to me, is very bright. But on either side, the line fades away rapidly into the Fog. I can tell at once, then, that the line slants back quite sharply from the center.

On the other hand, the Doctor has a slightly different appearance. As with the Merchant, I see only a Straight Line with a very bright center. On either side, the Doctor's line also fades into the Fog, but not as rapidly as the Merchant's line. Thus I can tell at once that the Doctor's line does not slant back as sharply. Because of the slight difference in brightness, I know that one shape is an Equilateral Triangle and that the other is a Pentagon.

—A. Square (Edwin Abbott), from *Life in Flatland*

The Eastern Coral Snake and the Scarlet King Snake

In the United States, there are two kinds of snakes that are red, black, and yellow. One is the eastern coral snake, the most poisonous of all North American snakes. The other is the harmless scarlet king snake.

It is not easy to tell the two snakes apart. Both grow to between two and four feet. Both have bands of bright red, black, and yellow; however, the coral snake has a blunt, black snout, while the king snake has a pointier, red snout.

As you can tell, these two kinds of snakes look very similar. If you see a red, black, and yellow banded snake, think carefully before getting close. The scarlet king snake can do you no harm, but the eastern coral snake may bite, and its venom can be lethal.

—Ryan Smith

PRACTICE AND APPLY

Thinking Like a Reader

1. How does the author explain the difference between the Doctor and the Merchant?

2. What similarities did the author point out between the coral snake and the king snake?

Thinking Like a Writer

3. How did the author of "Is a Doctor Like a Merchant?" organize his comparison?

4. What comparison and contrast words did the author use to compare the two snakes?

5. **Reading Across Texts** Compare the two literature models. Did the authors organize their comparisons in similar ways or in different ways? Explain your answer.

Features of Writing That Compares

GUIDELINES

In **writing that compares**, the writer often explains how two items or topics are like and unlike each other. Writing that compares:

► explains how two topics are **similar**.

► explains how two topics are **different**.

► uses **logical organization** to arrange facts and details.

► uses words of **comparison and contrast**.

► Similarities

Reread "Is a Doctor Like a Merchant?" by Edwin Abbott on page 88. What is the author comparing? What phrase does he use to show you that two items are similar?

> As with the Merchant, I see only a Straight Line with a very bright center.

The phrase "As with the Merchant," lets you know that the writer is pointing out a similarity between the Merchant and the Doctor.

► Differences

The author contrasts the Merchant's line and the Doctor's line. How can you tell when he is mentioning a difference?

> On either side, the Doctor's line also fades into the Fog, but not as rapidly as the Merchant's line.

The phrase "but not as rapidly as" points out a contrast, or difference.

▶ Logical Organization

When writing to compare, you should organize your facts and details in a logical way. One way is to move back and forth between two items, comparing details of each. Another way is to give all the details about one item in a paragraph and then all the details about the other in another paragraph. The sentence below shows the method the author uses to compare the Doctor and the Merchant.

> In the case of the Merchant, I see a Straight Line . . .

Does the writer move back and forth between the Doctor and the Merchant, or does he give all the details about one and then all the details about the other?

▶ Comparison and Contrast Words

When authors use comparison writing, they include words such as *like, both, also, too,* and *in the same way* to show how two things are similar. To show how two things differ, they use words and phrases such as *however, but, while, on the other hand,* and *in the case of.*

> On the other hand, the Doctor has a slightly different appearance.

What words did the author use to show that he was making a contrast, or showing a difference?

PRACTICE AND APPLY

Create a Features Chart

1. List the features of good comparison writing.

2. Reread "The Eastern Coral Snake and the Scarlet King Snake" by Ryan Smith on page 89.

3. Write one example of each feature in Ryan's writing.

4. Do you think that Ryan's essay is a good example of writing that compares? Explain why.

Features	Examples

Prewrite

Writing that compares can inform readers about how two people, places, things, or ideas are alike and different. Writing a comparison gives you the chance to describe two items or ideas. It also lets you contrast two items to show their differences.

Purpose and Audience

The purpose of writing that compares is to give your audience information about how two people, places, things, or ideas are like and unlike each other.

Before writing, think about your audience. Will your readers be your classmates and your teacher? How will you clearly explain to them how two things are alike, yet different?

Choose a Topic

Start by **brainstorming** a list of two items that have some things in common and some differences. Think about topics that would interest your audience.

Once you have chosen a topic from your brainstorming list, **explore ideas**. List the features or traits of each thing you will compare. Then use a chart or a diagram to organize your ideas.

Audience

In your journal, make a list of what your audience may already know about your topic. Then list what they will need to know.

Here is how I explored my ideas.

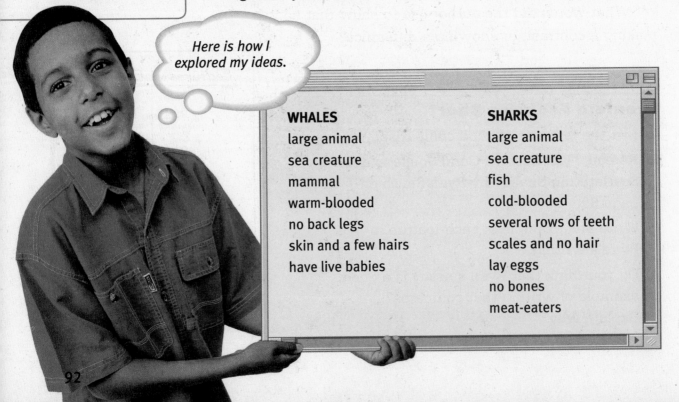

WHALES	SHARKS
large animal	large animal
sea creature	sea creature
mammal	fish
warm-blooded	cold-blooded
no back legs	several rows of teeth
skin and a few hairs	scales and no hair
have live babies	lay eggs
	no bones
	meat-eaters

Organize • Sorting

In writing that compares, writers sort, or classify, information. First, they think about the traits of each item. Next, they compare the two items for likenesses. Then, they think about the differences. Finally, they draw a conclusion about whether the two items are more alike than different. This writer organized the information from his list into a chart. Does his chart show that whales and sharks are more like or unlike each other? What ideas from his list did the writer decide not to put in his chart?

PREWRITE

DRAFT

REVISE

PROOFREAD

PUBLISH

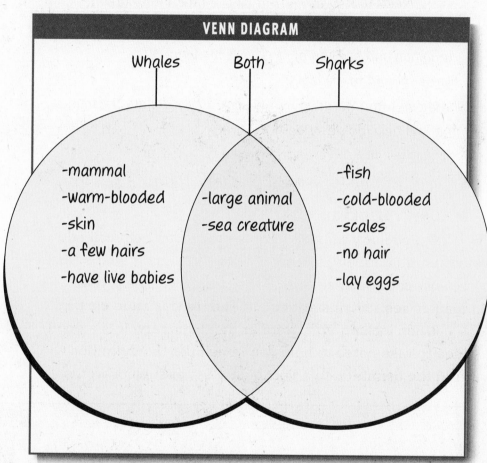

VENN DIAGRAM

Whales   Both   Sharks

-mammal
-warm-blooded
-skin
-a few hairs
-have live babies

-large animal
-sea creature

-fish
-cold-blooded
-scales
-no hair
-lay eggs

PRACTICE AND APPLY

Plan Your Writing That Compares

1. Think about your purpose and audience.

2. Brainstorm ideas for two items to compare.

3. Choose a topic and explore likenesses and differences.

4. Use a Venn diagram to compare and contrast.

Checklist ✓
Prewriting

- **Did you think about your purpose and audience?**

- **Did you choose a good topic and explore ideas?**

- **Did you make a list of traits, as well as lists of similarities and differences?**

- **Did you organize your information in a diagram or chart?**

- **Do you need to do any research?**

Prewrite • Research and Inquiry

▶ Writer's Resources

You may have to do research to get more information for your writing that compares. First, make a list of questions. Then decide what resources you will need to answer your questions. If you can, use technology in your research.

What Else Do I Need to Know?	Where Can I Find the Information?
Where can I find the definition and spelling of words related to my topic?	Look in a print or an online dictionary.
Where can I find words that will help me describe similarities and differences?	Look up words in a thesaurus.

▶ Use a Dictionary

A dictionary in book form or online can help you add accurate information to your writing. Defining words from science for a science topic, for example, can help your readers see the similarities and differences more clearly.

When looking up a word in the dictionary, it is a good idea to take notes to help you remember the definition. Add the definition to a vocabulary list of subject words.

The entry word is the highlighted

The definition shows the meaning of the word.

The pronunciation tells you how to say the word.

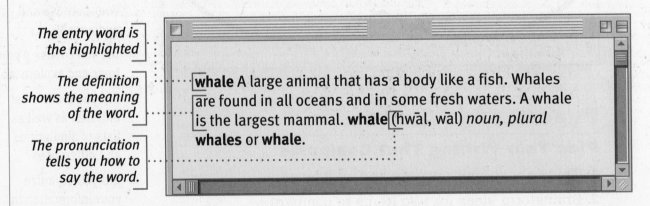

whale A large animal that has a body like a fish. Whales are found in all oceans and in some fresh waters. A whale is the largest mammal. **whale** (hwāl, wāl) *noun, plural* **whales** or **whale.**

▶ Use a Thesaurus

A thesaurus in book form or on a computer can help you choose the best words to describe or explain the similarities and differences between two items. A thesaurus lists words with the same or a similar meaning. These words are called *synonyms*. It also gives words with opposite meanings. These words are called *antonyms*. A thesaurus gives synonyms and antonyms for hundreds of words in the dictionary.

▶ Use Your Research

New information gathered from your research can be added to your chart. This writer found some new information. What did he add to his chart?

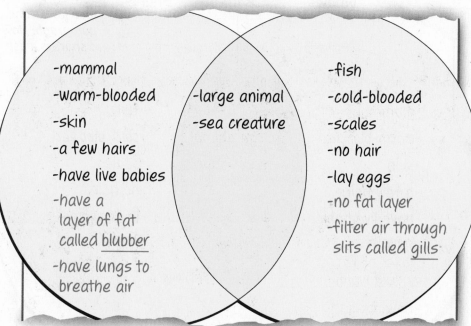

-mammal
-warm-blooded
-skin
-a few hairs
-have live babies
-have a layer of fat called blubber
-have lungs to breathe air

-large animal
-sea creature

-fish
-cold-blooded
-scales
-no hair
-lay eggs
-no fat layer
-filter air through slits called gills

PRACTICE AND APPLY

Review Your Plan

1. Look at your chart or diagram.

2. List questions you have about your topic.

3. Identify the resources you will need to find answers to your questions.

4. Add new information you gather to your chart.

Checklist ✓

Research and Inquiry

- ■ Did you list your questions?

- ■ Did you identify possible resources?

- ■ Did you take notes as you found information?

Draft

Before you begin writing your comparison, review your chart or diagram. Think about how you will organize your information. The *point-by-point* method is one way to organize. In this method, a writer moves back and forth between two items, giving similarities and differences of each. The *item-by-item* method is another way to organize information or details. In this method, the writer gives all the information about one item and then all the information about the other. Either method of organizing lets you present your information clearly.

✓ Checklist

Drafting

- Did you remember your purpose and audience? Did you make it clear in your introduction which two items you are comparing and why?

- Did you support the main idea of your topic with facts and details?

- Did you organize the information in a way that makes sense?

- Did you draw a conclusion based on the information you presented?

VENN DIAGRAM

Whales   Both   Sharks

Idea for first paragraph: How a whale is a mammal

Idea for second paragraph: How a shark is a fish

-mammal
-warm-blooded
-skin
-a few hairs
-have live babies
-have a layer of fat called blubber
-have lungs to breathe air

-large animal
-sea creature

-fish
-cold-blooded
-scales
-no hair
-lay eggs
-no fat layer
-filter air through slits called gills

Conclusion: More differences than similarities

Look at how this writer organized the information from his Venn diagram to write his comparison. He began by identifying the two things he chose to compare. Then he listed the features, or traits, of each thing, item by item.

PREWRITE

DRAFT

REVISE

PROOFREAD

PUBLISH

DRAFT

whales and sharks may seem alike, but their different in many ways. Altho both are large sea creatures, whales are mammals. Sharks are fish. As mammals, whales are warm blooded They have skin, a few hairs, and a layer of fat called blubber. Mammals also have lungs. Like other mammals, whales give birth to live babys.

Sharks are cold blooded. They also have scales rather than skin. Sharks have no hair or blubber. Like other fish, sharks filter air from water. They also lay eggs rather than give birth to live babies.

Though whales and large sharks are both sea creatures, they are different in many ways.

First sentence tells what is being compared

Shows how whales are mammals; orders information item by item

Shows how sharks are fish

Draws a conclusion based on information presented

PRACTICE AND APPLY

Draft Your Own Writing That Compares

1. Review your prewriting chart or diagram.
2. Decide between using the point-by-point or the item-by-item method of organizing your information.
3. Support important ideas with facts or details.
4. Draw a conclusion based on the information given.

TECHNOLOGY

Don't worry about making your work perfect when writing a first draft on the computer. Instead, focus on getting down your ideas. You'll have time to fix your errors later.

Revise

Elaborate

One way to improve your writing is to elaborate. When you elaborate, you add important ideas, facts, and details that may be missing from your writing. This writer added more details to expand the traits of whales.

> They have skin, a few hairs, and a layer of fat
> to control their body temperature
> called <u>blubber</u>.
> ^

The writer also elaborated on a difference between mammals and fish.

> to breathe air
> Mammals also have lungs.
> ^

> through their mouth and gills
> Like other fish, sharks filter air from water.
> ^

Word Choice

When you are writing, it is important to choose just the right words for your topic, type of writing, and audience.

When you are writing to compare, you need to find words that will help your readers understand how things are alike and different. You can use special words as clues to tell the reader you are showing a comparison (a likeness) or a contrast (a difference).

> On the other hand,
> Sharks are cold blooded. They also have scales
> ^
> In addition,
> rather than skin. Sharks have no hair or blubber. Like
> ^
> through their mouth and gills
> other fish, sharks filter air from water.
> ^

COMPARE AND CONTRAST WORDS

like
also
too
in addition
similarly
in the same way
both . . . and
different from
instead
however
although
unlike
but
yet
rather than
on the one hand
on the other hand
by contrast

Better Paragraphs

Regardless of the method you use to compare two items, each of your paragraphs should focus on a main idea, and all the paragraphs should flow together well. If you have chosen the item-by-item method, check to be sure you have used a separate paragraph for each item of your comparison. Read your paragraphs aloud. Have you grouped together the traits for one item in a paragraph and followed it with a paragraph of traits for the other item? Have you also used *analogies* to show how one thing is like another? For example, does the writer show an analogy between the lungs of a whale and the gills of a shark?

PREWRITE

DRAFT

REVISE

PROOFREAD

PUBLISH

As mammals, whales are warm blooded They have
            to control their body temperature
skin, a few hairs, and a layer of fat called blubber.
         to breathe air   ^
Mammals also have lungs. Like other mammals,
                          ^

whales give birth to live babys.
   On the other hand,
  ^Sharks are cold blooded. They also have scales
        In addition,
rather than skin. Sharks have no hair or blubber. Like
              ^   through their mouth and gills
other fish, sharks filter air from water.
                              ^

TECHNOLOGY

Does the word-processing program you are using provide a thesaurus? If so, use this feature to replace repeated or general words with more interesting and exact language.

PRACTICE AND APPLY

Revise Your Writing That Compares

1. Add facts or details to make clear how things are alike and different.

2. Organize your information by grouping it into paragraphs.

3. Use words that compare and contrast.

4. Grammar Did you use adjectives to provide descriptive details?

Writing PROCESS

Revise • Peer Conferencing

A partner can be of great help when you are revising your writing. Exchange papers with a partner. Then exchange ideas. Your partner may have some new ideas or suggestions that you haven't thought of yourself.

Good opening! ......

Add a contrast word. ....

What does "cold blooded" mean? ......

Make conclusion clearer by summarizing the differences. ....

whales and sharks may seem alike, but their different in many ways. Altho both are large sea creatures, whales are mammals. Sharks are fish. As mammals, whales are warm blooded They have skin, a few hairs, and a layer of fat called blubber. Mammals also have lungs. Like other mammals, whales give birth to live babys.

Sharks are cold blooded. They also have scales rather than skin. Sharks have no hair or blubber. Like other fish, sharks filter air from water. They also lay eggs rather than give birth to live babies.

Though whales and large sharks are both sea creatures, they are different in many ways.

TiP!

Conferencing for the Reader

■ Are features of writing that compares included in your partner's work?
- differences and similarities
- logical organization
- words that compare and contrast
- conclusion based on information presented

■ Discuss with your partner the parts of his or her draft that are effective as well as the parts that need revising.

When you revise your comparison-contrast writing, you will want to think about the comments and suggestions your partner made during your conference. This writer made some changes based on his partner's ideas.

PREWRITE

DRAFT

REVISE

PROOFREAD

PUBLISH

REVISE

Is a Shark Like a Whale?

whales and sharks may seem alike, but their

different in many ways. Altho both are large sea

~By contrast,~

creatures, whales are mammals. Sharks are fish. As

mammals, whales are warm blooded They have skin, a

~to control their body temperature~

few hairs, and a layer of fat called blubber. Mammals

~to breathe air.~

also have lungs. Like other mammals, whales give birth

to live babys. ~As fish, their body temperature~
~On the other hand,~ ~changes with ocean temperature.~

Sharks are cold blooded. They also have scales

~In addition,~

rather than skin. Sharks have no hair or blubber. Like

~through their mouth and gills~

other fish, sharks filter air from water. They also lay

eggs rather than give birth to live babies.

Though whales and large sharks are both sea

~how they look, breathe, have babies, and control body~

creatures, they are different in ~~many ways.~~ ~temperature.~

PRACTICE AND APPLY

Revise Your Writing That Compares

1. Read the notes from your peer conference.

2. Use these notes to improve your draft.

3. Add a title that will interest your audience.

4. Add more information, facts, and details that will make your writing clearer, more interesting, and more exact.

Checklist ✔

Revising

- Does your writing suit your purpose and audience?

- Do you need to elaborate on any ideas or details?

- Did you use words that compare and contrast?

- Did you organize your ideas in a way that makes sense?

- Did you write long and short sentences to add variety to your writing?

- Did you choose your words carefully?

- Did you write a conclusion that summarizes your information?

Writing PROCESS

Proofread/Edit

After you have revised your writing, you will need to proofread and edit it to find and correct any mistakes in mechanics, grammar and usage, and spelling.

STRATEGIES FOR PROOFREADING

- **Reread your revised draft several times.** Each time, look for a different type of error. You'll have a better chance of catching your errors that way.

- **Read each sentence for correct capitalization.** Remember that the first word of a sentence must begin with a capital letter.

- **Reread each paragraph for fluency.** Check to see if each paragraph has a main-idea sentence and facts or details that support it.

- **Read for mechanics and usage.** Be sure your writing has the correct punctuation, including apostrophes in contractions and correct end marks.

- **Check for spelling mistakes.** Use the dictionary or spell checker on the computer to help you.

TiP!

Spelling

When a root word, or base word, ends in a consonant and *y*, change the *y* to *i* when adding a plural (*-es*) ending (*baby* + *-es* = *babies*).

REVIEW THE RULES

GRAMMAR

- Many adjectives can be used to compare and contrast two or more people, places, things, or ideas by adding the endings *-er* and *-est*.

MECHANICS

- A hyphen is used to connect two or more words to form a compound word.

- A pronoun-verb contraction, such as *you're*, combines a pronoun (*you*) with a verb (*are*) to make a shortened form of two words. Do not confuse the possessive pronouns *your*, *its*, *their* with pronoun-verb contractions *you're*, *it's*, *they're*.

Go to pages 138–169 to review other rules.

Look at the proofreading corrections made on the draft below. What does the symbol SP mean? Why does the writer want to be sure that he spells his words correctly?

PROOFREAD

Is a Shark Like a Whale?

whales and sharks may seem alike, but their ~~they're~~ SP

SP Although

different in many ways. ~~Altho~~ both are large sea

By contrast,

creatures, whales are mammals. Sharks are fish. ⌗ As

mammals, whales are warm blooded They have skin, a

to control their body temperature

few hairs, and a layer of fat called blubber. Mammals

to breathe air.

also have lungs. Like other mammals, whales give birth

SP babies

to live ~~babys~~. As fish, their body temperature

changes with ocean temperature.

On the other hand,

Sharks are cold blooded. They also have scales

In addition,

rather than skin. Sharks have no hair or blubber. Like

through their mouth and gills·

other fish, sharks filter air from water. They also lay

eggs rather than give birth to live babies.

Though whales and (large) sharks are both sea

how they look, breathe, have babies, and control body

creatures, they are different in ~~many ways~~. temperature.

Checklist ✓

Proofreading

- ■ Did you indent each paragraph?

- ■ Did you use hyphens and end punctuation correctly?

- ■ Did you correct any mistakes in the use of comparative or superlative adjectives?

- ■ Did you spell all the words correctly?

PROOFREADING MARKS

⌗ new paragraph

∧ add

take out

≡ Make a capital letter.

/ Make a small letter.

SP Check the spelling.

⊙ Add a period.

PRACTICE AND APPLY

Proofread Your Writing That Compares

1. Be sure to indent paragraphs and to begin each sentence with a capital letter.

2. Correct any spelling errors.

3. Check for correct punctuation at the end of each sentence.

4. Correct any mistakes in the use of comparative and superlative adjectives.

Publish

Writing PROCESS

Before you publish your work, read through your writing one last time. Use a checklist to help you focus your efforts.

✓ Self-Check Writing That Compares

❑ Did I state my purpose clearly at the beginning?

❑ Who was my audience? Did I write in a way that will interest them?

❑ Did I organize my information in a way that makes sense?

❑ Did I include enough facts and details to show how two items are alike and different?

❑ Did I choose words to help compare and contrast?

❑ Did I base my conclusion on the facts I presented?

❑ Are my sentences varied? Do they flow together easily?

❑ Did I proofread and correct all errors?

This writer used the checklist to review his writing. Read "Is a Shark Like a Whale?" and discuss the writer's published piece. Is there anything you would have changed or added before publishing? What makes the writer feel that his draft is ready to publish? Do you think it is? Why do you think so?

Is a Shark Like a Whale?

by Simon Vega

Whales and sharks may seem alike, but they're different in many ways. Although both are large sea creatures, whales are mammals. By contrast, sharks are fish.

As mammals, whales are warm-blooded. They have skin, a few hairs, and a layer of fat called blubber to control their body temperature. Mammals also have lungs to breathe air. Like other mammals, whales give birth to live babies.

On the other hand, sharks are cold-blooded. As fish, their body temperature changes with ocean temperature. They also have scales rather than skin. In addition, sharks have no hair or blubber. Like other fish, sharks filter air from water through their mouth and gills. They also lay eggs rather than give birth to live babies.

Though whales and sharks are both large sea creatures, they are different in how they look, breathe, have babies, and control body temperature.

PRACTICE AND APPLY

Publish Your Writing That Compares

1. Check your revised draft one more time.
2. Copy your draft over neatly or print out a new copy.
3. Add pictures to show your comparisons.

TiP!

TECHNOLOGY

Does your school have a Web site? Use your school's technology resources to publish your work on the Internet.

Writing That Compares

Score	Description
4 Excellent	<ul><li>describes two items or topics by comparing and contrasting details</li><li>organizes the descriptions in a way that guides readers and includes a conclusion</li><li>uses a clear voice that shows detailed knowledge</li><li>uses precise compare and contrast words</li><li>uses a variety of sentences in which ideas flow smoothly</li><li>is free or almost free of errors</li></ul>
3 Good	<ul><li>describes items or topics by comparing and contrasting some details</li><li>organizes the comparison well and draws a conclusion</li><li>attempts to connect with readers in a voice that shows knowledge</li><li>uses compare and contrast words correctly</li><li>uses a variety of complete sentences</li><li>has minor errors that do not confuse the reader</li></ul>
2 Fair	<ul><li>description contains few details and is not clear</li><li>does not organize the descriptions clearly and has no conclusion</li><li>doesn't connect well with reader and shows incomplete knowledge</li><li>uses few compare and contrast words</li><li>writes choppy sentences that are hard to follow</li><li>makes frequent errors that confuse the reader</li></ul>
1 Unsatisfactory	<ul><li>does not adequately compare two items or topics</li><li>lacks organization or flow</li><li>shows little or no knowledge and confuses the reader</li><li>uses only general or vague words</li><li>uses run-on sentences and sentence fragments</li><li>makes serious and repeated errors</li></ul>

Go to www.macmillanmh.com for a 6-Point Student Writing Rubric.

Unit 6
Expository Writing: A How-To

Expository Writing: A How-To

Have you ever had to write down directions for someone? Have you ever had to explain how to do or make something? Your directions or instructions were an example of how-to writing. Writing that explains, or explanatory writing, tells an audience how to do something by giving step-by-step directions.

Learning from Writers

Read the following examples of how-to writing. What are the writers explaining? Notice the details that help you follow the steps of the explanation. As you read, look for spatial words that show location or distance.

THINK AND WRITE

Purpose

Why is it important to write a clear explanation? Write your ideas in your journal. Also tell why it is important to organize your steps in a logical way.

Can You Make a Rainbow?

Can you make a rainbow with a garden hose? If you've stood with your back to the sun and looked at the fine mist from a hose, fountain, or waterfall, you've probably seen a rainbow form.

You can also make a rainbow indoors. Fill a clear plastic cup about halfway with water. Carefully place it on the edge of a table. A third of it should extend over the edge. Hold a piece of white paper directly behind the cup. Shine a flashlight vertically through the bottom of the cup. You should see a rainbow on the paper.

—from *a science textbook*

An Unusual Vegetable

Last year I amazed my friends when I showed them a cucumber inside a bottle. They all wondered how I had managed to get it in there, as the vegetable was much too big to fit through the bottle's narrow neck. Here's how I did it.

In May, I planted some cucumber seeds about six inches apart from one another. Because a cucumber plant is a vine, it will grow up a fence; or it can also be tied with string to a stake as it grows. I used an old stepladder and planted seeds on both sides.

Soon the vines started to grow up the stepladder, and there were small cucumbers starting to form. I chose one about one inch long, but I did not pick it. I slipped the vegetable on its stalk into the bottle. Several weeks later, when the cucumber was fully grown, I cut the stalk and showed my cucumber in a bottle to my baffled friends.   —Adam Ling

PRACTICE AND APPLY

Thinking Like a Reader

1. Explain how to create a rainbow as described in "Can You Make a Rainbow?"

2. List in order the step-by-step directions for getting a cucumber inside a bottle as explained in "An Unusual Vegetable."

Thinking Like a Writer

3. What spatial words did the authors of "Can You Make a Rainbow?" include?

4. What time-order and spatial words did the author of "An Unusual Vegetable" use to organize his steps?

5. Reading Across Texts Compare the two literature models. Write about how they use step-by-step instructions to explain a task.

Features of How-to Writing

GUIDELINES

In how-to writing, the writer gives directions or tells the audience how to do or make something, step by step. Good explanatory writing:

▶ **explains** or gives information on how to complete a specific task.

▶ presents **step-by-step instructions** organized in a logical way.

▶ gives **clear details** that are easy to follow.

▶ uses **time-order words** or **spatial words** to make instructions clearer.

▶ Explains or Gives Information

Reread "Can You Make a Rainbow?" on page 108. What will you know how to do after reading the directions?

> Can you make a rainbow with a garden hose?

The main idea of each paragraph suggests that you will learn how to make a rainbow.

▶ Step-by-Step Instructions

Reread the second paragraph of "Can You Make a Rainbow?" What is the last step in making a rainbow indoors?

> Shine a flashlight vertically through the bottom of the cup.

The next-to-last sentence in the paragraph explains the last step. The last sentence in the paragraph tells what will happen if you complete all the steps of the process.

▶ Clear Details

Details give specific information about the steps the writer presents in explanatory writing. The sentence below gives details that help the audience understand what to do.

> Fill a clear-plastic cup about halfway with water.

Notice how the authors tell the exact kind of cup to use as well as how much water to place in the cup.

▶ Time-Order or Spatial Words

Time-order or spatial words help you clearly understand how to complete the steps of the process.

> Hold a piece of white paper directly behind the cup.

What spatial words tell you where to place the paper? How do these words make the instructions clearer and easier to follow?

PRACTICE AND APPLY

Create a Features Chart

1. List the features of good how-to writing.
2. Reread "An Unusual Vegetable" by Adam Ling on page 109.
3. Write one example of each feature in Adam's writing.
4. Write a brief summary of the information Adam gives. List the steps in order.

Features	Examples

Prewrite

Explanatory writing gives the reader facts and information about a topic. This writing is sometimes called "how-to" writing because it often explains how to make or do something. Writing an explanation gives you the chance to let others know how to do something that you know how to do.

Purpose and Audience

The purpose of explanatory writing is to inform your reader by giving clear step-by-step instructions. Before writing, think about your audience. Who will your readers be? Also, think about how to present your ideas. What words will you choose to make the steps of your explanation clear?

Choose a Topic

Begin by **brainstorming** a list of things you know how to do well and could explain to others. You might think about explaining a science experiment or another project.

Next, look at your list and choose a topic.

Then, **explore ideas** by making a list of the steps in the experiment or project. Later, you will organize these steps in a flowchart.

THiNK AND WRITE

Audience

How will your audience affect the way you explain how to do or make something? Write your ideas in your journal.

Here is my list of steps that will explain how to make frost.

How to Make Frost

The temperature needs to be cold.

Place ice in a plastic bag.

Add salt to keep ice cold.

Break ice into pieces.

Use ice pick or hammer.

Put layers of ice in a can.

Put layers of salt in the can.

Keep in a cool place.

Wait for an hour or two.

Watch the frost form on the can.

Organize • Sequence

Writing that explains usually presents instructions in a step-by-step order. To explain something step-by-step, you can use a flowchart to plan your writing. Not all your ideas may be needed, however. What ideas from the list did this writer leave out of her chart?

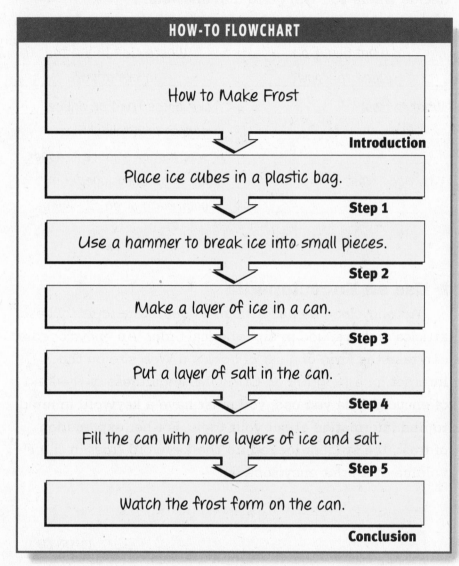

HOW-TO FLOWCHART

How to Make Frost

Introduction

Place ice cubes in a plastic bag.

Step 1

Use a hammer to break ice into small pieces.

Step 2

Make a layer of ice in a can.

Step 3

Put a layer of salt in the can.

Step 4

Fill the can with more layers of ice and salt.

Step 5

Watch the frost form on the can.

Conclusion

Checklist ✓
Prewriting

- Did you think about your purpose and audience?

- Did you make a list of the things you know how to do well?

- Did you choose an experiment, a project, or a skill that you can explain to others?

- Did you organize the steps of the experiment in a flowchart?

- Do you need to check facts or do any research?

PRACTICE AND APPLY

Plan Your Own Explanatory Writing

1. Think about your purpose and audience.

2. Brainstorm ideas for a topic to explain.

3. Choose an experiment, a project, or a skill and explore ideas.

4. Organize your ideas in a flowchart.

113

Writing PROCESS

Prewrite • Research and Inquiry

▶ Writer's Resources

You may need to do research to get more information for your explanation. First, make a list of questions. Then, decide where you will go to find answers.

What Else Do I Need to Know?	Where Can I Find the Information?
What is frost?	Take notes from an online search or a talk with a scientist or science teacher.
Why does frost form?	Look in an encyclopedia in book form or on CD-Rom.

▶ Use an Encyclopedia

An encyclopedia has articles about many topics. These articles are arranged in alphabetical order. An encyclopedia can take the form of a set of books, a Web site on the Internet, or a program on CD-ROM. Regardless of the kind of encyclopedia you use, you must have a keyword in mind to find information about your topic. For her explanation of frost, the student looked up the keyword *frost* in the *F* volume of a print encyclopedia.

Guide words help you find the article by giving the name of the first complete entry on the page.

The entry word is the title of the article. It is often the keyword of your topic.

A cross reference leads you to other articles that will give you more information.

FRONTIER

FRONTIER. See **PIONEER LIFE IN THE U.S**

FROST is one form of water. It is a pattern of ice crystals that forms when water vapor condenses on a surface, such as a windowpane. Frost usually occurs on cold, cloudless nights when the air temperature drops below 32°F. (0 C), the freezing point of water.

Frost and dew form in much the same way. At night, the drop in temperature causes the earth to cool. As the earth gets cooler, the water condenses, forming dewdrops on surfaces. Some of these dewdrops freeze when the temperature falls below freezing. When the frozen droplets get larger, they become frost crystals.

See also **DEW.**

▶ Search Online

National information services and online encyclopedias can help you check facts and find information. Search the Internet for these and other useful resources. Take notes or print out facts that will help you explain your topic. Write down the Web address for each piece of information you find.

▶ Use Your Research

Review your flowchart and add any new information you gained from your research. This writer discovered important information about how frost is made. How did she change the introduction and final steps on her chart?

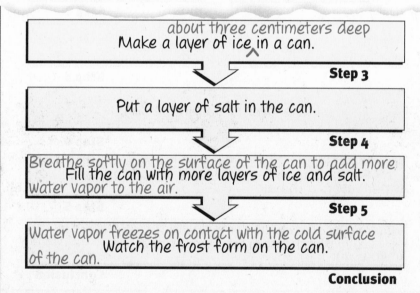

How to Make Frost
Frost is one form of water. It is made from water vapor.

Introduction

about three centimeters deep
Make a layer of ice in a can.

Step 3

Put a layer of salt in the can.

Step 4

Breathe softly on the surface of the can to add more
Fill the can with more layers of ice and salt.
water vapor to the air.

Step 5

Water vapor freezes on contact with the cold surface
Watch the frost form on the can.
of the can.

Conclusion

Checklist ✓

Research and Inquiry

- ■ Did you list your questions?

- ■ Did you identify possible resources?

- ■ Did you take notes or print out useful information?

PRACTICE AND APPLY

Review Your Plan

1. Look at your flowchart.

2. List questions you have about your topic.

3. Identify the resources you will need to find answers.

115

Draft

Before you begin writing your explanation, review the flowchart you made. Think about making a paragraph for your introduction, for the steps in the middle of your draft, and for your conclusion. Include details that support your step-by-step explanation.

HOW-TO FLOWCHART

How to Make Frost
Frost is one form of water. It is made from water vapor.

Introduction

The first paragraph should explain what I am going to show how to make.

Place ice cubes in a plastic bag.

Step 1

Use a hammer to break ice into small pieces.

Step 2

The steps will make a good second paragraph. I may need to add details to make the steps clearer.

about three centimeters deep
Make a layer of ice in a can.

Step 3

Put a layer of salt in the can.

Step 4

Breathe softly on the surface of the can to add more water vapor to the air.
Fill the can with more layers of ice and salt.

Step 5

Water vapor freezes on contact with the cold surface of the can.
Watch the frost form on the can.

Conclusion

The last paragraph should show what will happen if I follow all the steps.

✓ Checklist

Drafting

- Does your explanation fit your purpose and audience?

- Are the steps organized in the right order?

- Have you included all the steps so that your audience can do the experiment?

- Do you need to add any important information or details?

- Do you begin and end your explanation in an interesting way?

Look at how this writer used the ideas on her chart to write a first draft. She opened with a question that would get her readers' attention. Then she used time-order words to help show the steps her audience would need to follow in order to do the experiment.

PREWRITE

DRAFT

REVISE

PROOFREAD

PUBLISH

DRAFT

Have you ever notised the frost that forms on windows in the Winter? Did you know that you can make frost? frost was one form of water. It is made from another form of water called water vapor.

First paragraph tells what the audience will learn how to make.

First place ice cubes in a plastic bag. Use a hammer to break the cubes into small pieces. Next make a layer of ice about three centimeters deep in a can. Then add a thin layer of salt. Repeat layers of ice and salt until the can is full The surrounding air must contain water vapor for frost to form. Finally, breathe softly on the surface of the can to add more water vapor to the air.

Second paragraph explains how to do this experiment. Time-order words connect the steps.

Watch as frost appears on the can. The frost form when the water vapor freezes on contact with the cold surface of the can.

Third paragraph states the conclusion.

PRACTICE AND APPLY

Draft Your Own Explanatory Writing

1. Review your prewriting flowchart.
2. Write about how to make or do something.
3. Put the steps of the experiment in order and use time-order words.
4. Tell the outcome of the experiment in the conclusion.

TECHNOLOGY

You can use the cut-and-paste feature on your computer to put the steps of your explanation in a better order.

Revise

Elaborate

One way to improve your writing is to elaborate. When you elaborate, you add important ideas and details that you might have left out. When you revise your writing, you may need to explain in more detail.

The writer changed some of her directions to make them easier to follow.

> *and seal tightly*
> First place ice cubes in a plastic bag.

The writer added a better description of where to place the first layer of ice.

> *place*
> Next make a layer of ice about three centimeters
> *at the bottom of*
> deep in a can.

Word Choice

When you are writing, it is important to choose just the right words for your topic and audience.

In an explanation, you need to use spatial words that will help your reader do exactly what is needed to complete each step.

> *inside*   *and seal tightly*
> First place ice cubes in a plastic bag. Use a hammer
> *place*
> to break the cubes into small pieces. Next make a
> *at the bottom of*
> layer of ice about three centimeters deep in a can.
> *on top of the ice*
> Then add a thin layer of salt. Repeat layers of ice
> and salt until the can is full

SPATIAL WORDS

inside
outside
next to
through
on top of
at the bottom of
above
below
near
far
across

Better Sentences

As you continue to revise your draft, check the way your sentences sound. Read them aloud. Do your subjects and verbs agree?

When you check for subject-verb agreement in your writing, find the subject of the sentence first. Then find the predicate, or the verb, of the sentence. Remember: If the subject is singular, the verb must be singular. If the subject is plural, the verb must be plural. Add -s to most verbs if the subject is singular in the present tense.

> forms
> The frost ~~form~~ when the water vapor freezes on
> contact with the cold surface of the can.

PRACTICE AND APPLY

Revise Your Own Explanatory Writing

1. Add details or information that will make it easier for your reader to do the activity.

2. Use spatial words to help your reader understand the process.

3. Add details or information that will make your writing clearer and more interesting.

4. **Grammar** Check for subject-verb agreement in your explanatory writing. Also check that adverbs and adjectives are used properly.

TECHNOLOGY

Some of your classmates may know word-processing tips that you might like to know. Ask them to explain and demonstrate these tips by using steps that you can understand.

Revise • Peer Conferencing

Take a break from your writing. Exchange drafts with a partner. Your partner may have some good suggestions to give you. Remember: If your partner can't follow your steps, your audience probably won't be able to follow them either.

Writing PROCESS

Your question gets me interested right away.

What materials do you need?

Time-order words help me see the steps.

Add another word to connect the last paragraph.

Have you ever notised the frost that forms on windows in the Winter? Did you know that you can make frost? frost was one form of water. It is made from another form of water called water vapor.

First place ice cubes in a plastic bag. Use a hammer to break the cubes into small pieces. Next make a layer of ice about three centimeters deep in a can. Then add a thin layer of salt. Repeat layers of ice and salt until the can is full The surrounding air must contain water vapor for frost to form. Finally, breathe softly on the surface of the can to add more water vapor to the air.

Watch as frost appears on the can. The frost form when the water vapor freezes on contact with the cold surface of the can.

TiP!

Conferencing for the Reader

■ Are features of explanatory writing included in your partner's writing?

- informs or explains
- step-by-step instructions
- clear details
- time-order and spatial words

■ Make sure to tell your partner what's good about the piece as well as what needs improvement.

When you revise your explanatory writing, consider your partner's comments. This writer made changes based on her partner's ideas.

REVISE

How to Make Frost

Have you ever notised the frost that forms on windows in the Winter? Did you know that you can make frost? frost was one form of water. It is made All you need are ice cubes, a plastic bag, a hammer, an empty coffee can, from another form of water called water vapor. and salt.

inside and seal tightly.

First place ice cubes in a plastic bag. Use a hammer to break the cubes into small pieces. Next ~~make~~ place a layer of at the bottom of ice about three centimeters deep in a can. Then add a on top of the ice thin layer of salt. Repeat layers of ice and salt until the can is full The surrounding air must contain water vapor for frost to form. Finally, breathe softly on the surface of the can to add more water vapor to the air.

Now Watch as frost appears on the can. The frost ~~form~~ forms when the water vapor freezes on contact with the cold surface of the can.

Checklist ✓

Revising

■ Does your explanation suit your purpose and audience?

■ Do you need to elaborate on any of your steps?

■ Did you describe each of your steps clearly?

■ Did you use spatial words to make your steps clearer?

■ Did you write your steps in the correct order?

■ Did you add a good title?

PRACTICE AND APPLY

Revise Your Own Writing That Explains

1. Read your notes from the peer conference.

2. Add information that will make your steps clearer.

3. Take out information from your draft that isn't necessary.

4. Add a clear, simple title.

Proofread/Edit

After you have revised your explanatory writing, you will need to proofread and edit it to find and correct any errors in mechanics, grammar and usage, and spelling.

Writing PROCESS

STRATEGIES FOR PROOFREADING

- **Read your revised explanation several times, each time looking for a different type of error.** This will give you a better chance of catching all mistakes.

- **Read each sentence again to make sure that nouns, verbs, pronouns, adverbs and adjectives are used properly.** Make sure that they all agree in tense and number.

- **Reread for mechanics and usage.** Make sure that your writing is clear and makes sense.

- **Check for spelling mistakes.** Use a dictionary or the spell checker on your computer.

Spelling

When *c* represents the /s/ sound, *c* is always followed by *e*, *i*, or *y*, as in *noticed*.

REVIEW THE RULES

GRAMMAR

- **Present-tense** verbs tell that something is happening now.

- **Past-tense** verbs tell that something has already happened.

- **Future-tense** verbs tell that something is going to happen.

- Be sure that subjects and verbs agree.

- Add *-s* or *-es* to form most singular verbs in the present.

- Add *-d* or *-ed* to form the past tense of many verbs.

MECHANICS

- Use a **comma** after a time-order word, such as *first, next,* and *finally,* and to separate three or more items in a series.

Go to pages 138–169 to review other rules.

Look at the proofreading corrections made on the draft below. What does the symbol ⨎ mean? Why does the writer want to start a new paragraph?

PREWRITE

DRAFT

REVISE

PROOFREAD

PUBLISH

PROOFREAD

How to Make Frost

Have you ever notised the frost that forms on windows in the Winter? Did you know that you can make frost? frost was one form of water. It is made from another form of water called water vapor. All you need are ice cubes, a plastic bag, a hammer, an empty coffee can, and salt.

⨎First, place ice cubes in a plastic bag. inside and seal tightly. Use a hammer to break the cubes into small pieces. Next, make a layer of place ice about three centimeters deep in a can. at the bottom of Then, add a thin layer of salt. on top of the ice Repeat layers of ice and salt until the can is full. The surrounding air must contain water vapor for frost to form. Finally, breathe softly on the surface of the can to add more water vapor to the air.

Now Watch as frost appears on the can. The frost form forms when the water vapor freezes on contact with the cold surface of the can.

Checklist ✓
Proofreading

- Did you spell all the words correctly?

- Did you insert commas after time-order words?

- Did you correct any problems with verb tenses?

- Did you end each sentence with the correct punctuation mark?

- Did you indent each paragraph?

PROOFREADING MARKS

⨎ new paragraph

∧ add

take out

≡ Make a capital letter.

/ Make a small letter.

(SP) Check the spelling.

⊙ Add a period.

PRACTICE AND APPLY

Proofread Your Own Explanatory Writing

1. Correct spelling mistakes.

2. Add missing commas.

3. Correct problems with verb tenses. Check the forms of adverbs and adjectives.

4. Indent paragraphs.

Publish

Before you publish, review your writing one more time. Use a checklist to help you focus on your work.

✓ Self-Check   Explanatory Writing

- ❑ Who was my audience? Did I write in a way that will interest them?
- ❑ What was my purpose? Will my audience understand my explanation?
- ❑ Did I write a strong introduction and conclusion?
- ❑ Did I present my steps in the right order?
- ❑ Did I choose the best spatial and time-order words to make my instructions clear?
- ❑ Are my sentences varied? Do they fit together well?
- ❑ Did I use verb tenses and subject-verb agreement correctly?
- ❑ Did I use commas correctly?
- ❑ Did I proofread my writing and correct all the errors?

This writer used the checklist to review her explanation. Read "How to Make Frost," and discuss the writer's published work. Do you think her writing was ready to publish? Why do you think so?

How to Make Frost

by Emily Chambers

Have you ever noticed the frost that forms on windows in the winter? Did you know that you can make frost? Frost is one form of water. It is made from another form of water called water vapor. All you need are ice cubes, a plastic bag, a hammer, an empty coffee can, and salt.

First, place ice cubes inside a plastic bag and seal tightly. Use a hammer to break the cubes into small pieces. Next, place a layer of ice about three centimeters deep at the bottom of a can. Then, add a thin layer of salt on top of the ice. Repeat layers of ice and salt until the can is full. The surrounding air must contain water vapor for frost to form. Finally, breathe softly on the surface of the can to add more water vapor to the air.

Now watch as frost appears on the can. The frost forms when the water vapor freezes on contact with the cold surface of the can.

TECHNOLOGY

Experiment with different type fonts for your title. Be sure to use a large font size and a style that suits your subject.

PRACTICE AND APPLY

Publish Your Own Explanatory Writing

1. Check your revised draft one more time.
2. Print out or write a neat, final copy of your revised draft.
3. Add pictures that show the steps you have explained.

How-to Writing

Score	Description
4 Excellent	■ creates a focused explanation with clear details ■ explains the topic in an engaging manner and logical order ■ uses a personal style and shows original knowledge ■ uses spatial and time-order words ■ uses a variety of simple and complex sentences that flow smoothly ■ is free or almost free of errors
3 Good	■ creates a solid explanation with clear details ■ introduces the topic and presents steps in a logical order ■ uses a personal tone and shows knowledge of the topic ■ includes some spatial and time-order words ■ uses a variety of easy-to-follow sentences ■ has minor errors that do not confuse the reader
2 Fair	■ attempts an explanation, but details may be unclear ■ presents some steps out of order ■ does not connect to readers with enthusiasm ■ includes few spatial or time-order words ■ uses only simple sentences that lack variety ■ makes frequent errors that confuse the reader
1 Unsatisfactory	■ creates an incomplete explanation ■ does not include a clear beginning and presents steps illogically ■ does not use a personal voice and shows little knowledge of the topic ■ uses no spatial or time-order words and language not connected to the purpose ■ uses run-on sentences and sentence fragments ■ makes serious and repeated errors

Go to www.macmillanmh.com for a 6-Point Student Writing Rubric.

Main Idea and Details

A writer usually states the main idea of a paragraph in a topic sentence. The other sentences in the paragraph add details to develop or support the main idea.

GUIDELINES

- The **main idea** tells what a piece of writing is about.

- The main idea is usually stated in a **topic sentence**.

- In a **paragraph**, all the sentences should work together to support one main idea.

- **Detail sentences** support the main idea by giving examples, concrete details, facts, or opinions.

- Organize the main idea and supporting details in a **logical order**.

- Use **time-order words**, such as *first, next*, and *finally*, to connect ideas and to show the order, or sequence, of events.

THINK AND WRITE

Main Idea
Why is it important for a paragraph to have a main idea? Explain your answer in your journal.

Read this paragraph about a personal experience. Notice that the writer states the main idea and uses supporting details to develop that idea and make it clearer.

The topic sentence states the main idea of the paragraph.

A supporting detail helps to develop the main idea or make it clearer.

A time-order word helps to connect ideas and show the order of events.

I met my best friend Ashley in an unusual way. On the first day of summer vacation, Ashley and her family moved into the house next door. The day after they moved in, she and her brother were playing catch in their front yard. Ashley threw the ball too hard, and it sailed over her brother's head, right through my bedroom window! After that surprising introduction, we became best friends. Now we all play ball almost every day. However, these days we do our best to avoid windows.

128

Leads and Endings

To focus a reader's attention, to persuade an audience to do something, or to draw a reader into a story, writers begin with a strong lead. A lead is the opening in a piece of writing. Its purpose is to "grab" the reader's attention. In the same way, endings must also be strong. An ending is the closing in a piece of writing. It summarizes the piece or draws a conclusion. It may even leave the audience with something to think about.

GUIDELINES

- A **lead** is at the beginning of a piece of writing.

- A lead can use an **"attention-getter,"** such as a question, a quotation, an anecdote, or a humorous brief story.

- A lead can include the writer's **main idea**.

- An **ending** is the last part of a piece of writing.

- An ending can **summarize** the piece or draw a **conclusion**. It can leave the reader with a question or with the feeling that it has tied up all the loose ends.

THINK AND WRITE

Leads and Endings

Why is it important for a newspaper article to have a strong lead? Write your ideas in a brief paragraph.

Read the paragraph. Notice how the author's lead and ending help the reader focus on the main ideas.

We've got to take that trip to Monterey! Our family would enjoy Monterey Bay. We all love to sail, and the bay and the wharf in Monterey are terrific. We could drive, and that would be less expensive than flying. Besides, Dad said that he wanted us to see where he grew up. I think a trip to Monterey would be the perfect family vacation for us.

This lead makes the reader want to find out about the trip.

The ending summarizes the main idea of the paragraph.

Organization

To produce a well-organized paragraph, writers must arrange their sentences in a clear and logical order. This means that all sentences in a paragraph will relate to the main idea.

GUIDELINES

- **Organization** in a paragraph shows a clear and logical connection of ideas.

- A **well-organized paragraph** presents sentences in a logical order.

- Two ways to **organize information** are by time order and spatial order.

- **Time order** uses words such as *first, next,* and *then* to show the order in which an activity should be done.

- **Spatial order** uses words such as *above, near, over, beside, next to,* and *on top of* to make directions clearer.

Organization

Why is it important for a paragraph to be organized in a clear and logical way? Write a brief paragraph to explain your ideas.

Read this explanation. Notice how the writer uses time-order words and spatial words to organize steps to make them clearer and easier to understand.

All sentences in the paragraph are organized around the main idea.

Time-order words help organize the paragraph by listing the steps in order.

Spatial words make the steps easier to follow.

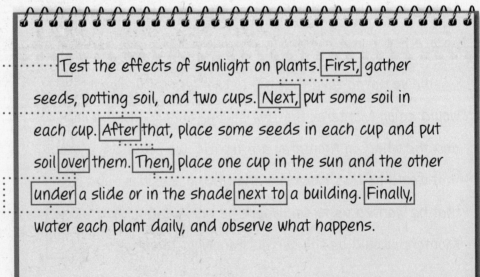

Test the effects of sunlight on plants. First, gather seeds, potting soil, and two cups. Next, put some soil in each cup. After that, place some seeds in each cup and put soil over them. Then, place one cup in the sun and the other under a slide or in the shade next to a building. Finally, water each plant daily, and observe what happens.

Outlining

Writers make outlines as a way to organize their main ideas and put their ideas in order.

GUIDELINES

- An **outline** is a plan that organizes ideas about a specific topic.

- Outlines **group facts into related categories**.

- An outline can be used to plan the **introduction**, **body**, and **conclusion** of a piece of writing.

- Use **Roman numerals** to list **main ideas** and **capital letters** to list the **supporting details** below each main idea.

- Use a **variety of sources** to find facts and details for your outline.

THINK AND WRITE

Outlining
Why is it important to know how to make an outline? List three reasons in your journal.

Look at the outline of the life of William Clark. Clark was one of the explorers who took part in the Lewis and Clark expedition. Notice how the writer organizes the ideas.

William Clark

I.   Clark's Early Life ....

   A. Born in Virginia in 1770

II. Lewis and Clark Expedition (1804–1806) ....

   A. Explored Louisiana Purchase with Meriwether Lewis

   B. Mapped routes, kept journal, made sketches

   C. Helped hire Sacajawea, a Shoshone guide

   D. Gathered materials and published records of journey

III. Clark's Later Years

   A. Became governor of the Missouri Territory ....

Each Roman numeral shows a main idea.

Each main idea will become a paragraph in the report.

A capital letter indicates a supporting detail.

Writing Description

A good description creates a clear, vivid picture of something or someone. It includes details that appeal to the reader's senses and organizes these details logically.

GUIDELINES

- A written description creates a clear and vivid picture of a person, place, or thing.

- Descriptive writing uses sensory details to appeal to the reader's sense of sight, hearing, smell, taste, and touch.

- Use word choice and exact and vivid language to pinpoint exactly how something looks, sounds, smells, tastes, and feels.

- In a description, the details should add up to an overall impression of the subject.

- Organize a description from bottom to top or by using some other spatial order, by presenting important details first or last, or by grouping together similar types of details.

THINK AND WRITE

Writing Dialogue

Why is it important for descriptive writing to be both interesting and accurate? Write your ideas in your journal.

Read this description of winter weather. Notice how the writer compares March in Minnesota to March in Kentucky by grouping together similar types of details.

Sensory details help the reader see a picture.

Vivid adjectives pinpoint exactly how something looks.

The details add up to an overall impression of how spring differs in Minnesota and Kentucky.

It was late March when we moved from Minnesota to Kentucky. In Minnesota, the ground was still blanketed with snow. It was the wet, dirty kind of snow that blends in with the slate gray March sky and the spindly trees. The Minnesota air was cold and damp as we loaded into the car.

In Kentucky, however, it felt like spring. We saw green grass and even some flowers peeking out of the ground. Unlike Minnesota, Kentucky is warm and colorful in March.

Dialogue

Dialogue is the written conversation between two or more characters in a story. It can also show what a character is thinking.

GUIDELINES

- **Dialogue** is the exact words that characters speak in a story.

- **Dialogue** describes characters and moves along the action of the story.

- Add **quotation marks** around a speaker's exact words.

- Add **details** to tell *who* is speaking and *how*.

- Use a **comma** to separate phrases such as *he said* or *she said* from the quotation itself.

- Place a comma or a period **inside closing quotation marks**.

- Begin the first word of dialogue with a **capital letter**.

- Begin a **new paragraph** each time the speaker changes.

THINK AND WRITE

Dialogue

How can you identify the speaker when you read dialogue in a story? Write a brief explanation in your journal.

Notice how the writer uses dialogue to help you get to know the characters and to move along the story's action.

A dog had chased my cat, Bubbles, under the porch, and the poor cat was too scared to leave. All afternoon, my neighbor Jim and I tried to coax her from her hiding place.

"Show her a cat toy," Jim suggested.

"I did, but she wasn't even interested," I replied glumly.

"Hey, I know what to do!" Jim cried. He fetched a can of cat food and held it out toward Bubbles. As soon as she heard the sound of the can opening, Bubbles crawled toward us.

"No cat can hold out for dinner!" Jim sang happily.

Dialogue is the exact words that a character speaks.

A new paragraph is used each time the speaker changes.

Quotation marks show a speaker's exact words.

Details tell who is speaking and how he or she is speaking.

Writing

Poem

A **poem** is a form of writing that allows you to express yourself.

*The **title** of a poem tells what the poem is about. Be sure to capitalize the first letter of each important word in the title.*

*A poem can be about any **topic**, but many poems are about nature.*

> Spring Is Full of Wonders
>
> Spring is full of wonders.
> Sometimes it is as mysterious as a little girl
> Who doesn't want to talk,
> Sometimes as simple and familiar as a
> garden fence.
> Or like old apple trees blossoming from
> time immemorial
> Or like a blue swallow returning under
> the eaves.
> Sometimes happy
> Sometimes sad
> But always interesting.
> Spring as usual,
> Common and familiar.
> However never repeating itself completely.
>   —Gordana Danicic

*This poem uses similes. A **simile** compares two unlike things by using the words like or as.*

*This poem uses **sensory words** to describe what the poet saw and felt.*

GUIDELINES

- Choose a **topic** that you would like to write about.
- Give your poem a **title**.
- Think of ways to use **sound** in your poem. Will it rhyme? Will it use repeated consonant or vowel sounds? Will it imitate a sound?
- Think about the pattern, or **form**, of your poem. Your poem can have a certain shape or be divided into stanzas, for example.

Practice Observe the world around you. What do you see and hear? Choose a topic that interests you. Then write your own poem.

Humorous Play

A **humorous play** tells an amusing story through dialogue, characters, stage directions, and props.

Writing

<u>Cinderella Meets Snow White</u> ·········· *A play needs a "catchy" title.*

<u>Characters</u>
CINDY: An 11-year-old girl ················ *A list of characters includes a brief description of each one.*
SNOW: An 11-year-old girl
PRINCE: An 11-year-old boy

Setting: A sunny day on a fairy-tale street ········ *The setting tells when and where the story takes place.*

Props: a hand mirror ·········

Scene 1:

Prince is in the center of the street practicing some dance steps. Cindy and Snow enter. ········· *Props and costumes are important to the story line.*

SNOW: Prince, is it true you're taking Cindy to the dance tonight?

CINDY: I heard you asked Snow to the dance. Is that true?

PRINCE: Well, it's like this, I . . .

SNOW: Why wouldn't he ask me? Watch this. *(Speaking to her hand mirror)* Mirror, ········· *Stage directions are included whenever you want the characters to perform any physical action.*
mirror in my hand, who's the fairest in the land? *(She gets no response.)* Mirror? Come in, mirror. I must have a bad connection.

CINDY: Have you thought of getting cable?

SNOW: Well, Prince, who is it going to be?

PRINCE: Well, um . . .

CINDY: Wait a minute. Why are we arguing ····· *The dialogue is the characters' spoken words.*
over him?

SNOW: You're right. Who wants a guy who can't keep his word?

PRINCE: Well, now wait a minute. I . . .

SNOW: *(Speaking to Cindy as they walk off together)* I'll meet you at 7:00.

PRINCE: Wait! Girls?? Somebody?? Yipes!!

Practice Write a humorous play based on a familiar story. Include the setting, plot, characters, dialogue, and stage directions.

Writing

Friendly Letter

A **friendly letter** is a letter that you would write to a friend or a family member. The tone of a friendly letter is familiar and casual. A friendly letter has these parts:

The heading gives the address of the person writing the letter.

2245 Beacon Street
Providence, Rhode Island 02906
January 23, 20__

Dear Amy,

The greeting begins with Dear and includes the name of the person to whom the letter is written.

Hi! How are you? Is it snowing in Providence? It snowed here last night. We had almost two inches of snow! My brother and I went outside this morning to build a snowman, but the snow had already turned to rain. Instead, we got out a puzzle and went to work.

The body is the main part of the letter.

When we got to the last piece, we couldn't find it. It turns out that Shep, our dog, had snatched it off the table and chewed it. We took the puzzle apart and put it away.

Tonight we're going to the mall to look for a new desk. The desk in my room is nice, but it's so small that I can't spread out my schoolbooks. I hope I can find a yellow one like yours.

Are you still coming to visit this summer? I'm excited that we'll be going to the water park. We'll have a great time! I hope to hear from you soon.

The closing is a way of saying good-bye. It is followed by a comma.

Your friend,

The signature is the signed name of the writer.

Julia

Practice Write a letter to a friend or a relative. Describe something you did on your last vacation, or an interesting hobby that you have. Be sure to include the correct letter form.

Editorial

An **editorial** is a form of writing that expresses a writer's opinion about a topic. Editorials are usually found in newspapers or magazines.

Bat Alert!

The Indiana Bat is in danger! In 1967, these flying mammals were added to the list of endangered species. Unfortunately, logging in our area has caused the Indiana Bat population to drop by 60% since the 1960s. Although some logging in nearby counties has been put on hold, everyone knows that the number of bats will continue to decrease until all logging in the area is stopped.

The only way to save these innocent creatures is to work together to help preserve their natural habitat. Otherwise, the Indiana Bat will surely vanish from the face of the earth.

State your opinion in a *topic sentence*.

Support your opinion with *facts* and *details*.

Use *opinion words* to convince your audience.

Save your *strongest argument* for last.

GUIDELINES

- Brainstorm a list of topics about which you have a strong opinion.
- Think about your audience. Will your classmates read your editorial? Will the community read it?
- Consider your purpose for writing. Are you writing to persuade?
- Research your topic. Use reference sources.
- Organize your ideas in a logical order.

Practice Think of an issue that concerns you, such as building parks, keeping streams clean, or recycling. Research information and write your own editorial.

Writing

Grammar

RULE 1 — Sentences and Sentence Fragments

- A **sentence** is a group of words that expresses a complete thought.

  The children went on a picnic.

- A **sentence fragment** is a group of words that does not express a complete thought.

  The boy in the red jacket. (needs a predicate)

  Carried the largest basket. (needs a subject)

Practice Write *sentence* or *fragment* for each group of words. Rewrite each fragment to make a complete sentence.

1. Began to fall.
2. The sky was filled with clouds.
3. We picked up our picnic supplies.
4. The entire group of friends into a shelter.
5. Picnic in the shelter.

RULE 2 — Types of Sentences

- There are four different types of sentences.

Type of Sentence	Examples
A **declarative sentence** makes a statement and ends with a period.	*Sue goes to the lake often.* *The beach was crowded with people.*
An **interrogative sentence** asks a question and ends with a question mark.	*Have you been there this year?* *Can Tom give me directions?*
An **imperative sentence** tells or asks someone to do something and ends with a period.	*Let me borrow your rowboat.* *Push the boat into the water.*
An **exclamatory sentence** expresses strong feeling and ends with an exclamation mark.	*Wow, what a beautiful day!* *Oh, no, I dropped the oar!*

Practice Write each sentence. Add the correct end punctuation. Write whether the sentence is *declarative*, *interrogative*, *imperative*, or *exclamatory*.

1. Have you ever been sailing

2. I took lessons last summer

3. Hey, it was the easiest thing I've ever learned

4. Hold this rope tightly

5. Don't let it slip through your hands

6. Oops, I almost tipped over

7. Do you want to steer for a while

8. The lesson lasts for one hour

9. Does it cost much money

10. Lessons are not very expensive

Compound Sentences

• A compound sentence contains two simple sentences that have similar ideas. They are joined by a comma and the word *and*, *or*, or *but*.

> *We went hiking, and the rain slowed us down.*

> *You can carry your pack, or they can carry it for you.*

> *Hiking is hard work, but I enjoy the exercise.*

Practice Combine each pair of sentences by using a comma and the word *and*, *but*, or *or* to create a compound sentence.

1. The trail is long. We should finish in two hours.

2. We can follow the trail. We could take a short cut.

3. It began to rain. The wind began to howl.

4. I saw bear tracks. I didn't see a bear.

5. We can stop here. We can eat lunch at the top.

 QUICK WRITE Write five compound sentences. Use the proper punctuation for each one.

Grammar

RULE 4

Complete Subjects and Complete Predicates

- The complete subject of a sentence includes all the words that tell *whom* or *what* the sentence is about.
- The complete predicate of a sentence includes all the words that tell what the subject *does* or *is*.

The new museum opens at nine o'clock.

Complete subject: The new museum

Complete predicate: opens at nine o'clock.

Practice **Write each sentence. Draw one line under the complete subject. Draw two lines under the complete predicate.**

1. Hector's class went to the museum.

2. All of the children were excited about the trip.

3. The tour guides taught them a lot about ancient times.

4. They studied pottery that was thousands of years old.

5. The boys and girls learned about the people who made the pottery.

RULE 5

Simple Subjects and Simple Predicates

- The simple subject is the main word in the complete subject. It tells exactly whom or what the sentence is about.

The helpful volunteer showed us a movie.

- The simple predicate is the main verb in the complete predicate. It tells exactly what the subject does or is.

All of the students thought that the movie was interesting.

Grammar

Practice Write each sentence. Draw one line under the simple subject and two lines under the simple predicate.

1. Many paintings hang on the walls.
2. Picasso painted in a unique style.
3. My favorite painting is the one by Picasso.
4. The colors glow under the lights.
5. The museum offers painting lessons.
6. The next class begins tomorrow.
7. I like my art class.
8. The instructor teaches about the artists.
9. He shows us many colors.
10. New art classes start every month.

 RULE 6

Compound Subjects & Compound Predicates

- A **compound subject** has two or more simple subjects that share the same predicate and are joined by the word *and* or *or*.

  *Stewart and Laura **went to the museum**.*

- A **compound predicate** has two or more simple predicates that share a subject and are joined by the word *and* or *or*.

  *We **stopped and visited** the insect exhibits.*

Practice Write each pair of sentences as one sentence with a compound subject or a compound predicate.

1. Spiders were on display. Insects were on display.
2. The tarantula has eight legs. The tarantula has a hairy body.
3. Stewart observes the beetles. Stewart takes notes on the beetles.
4. A boy notices the colorful butterfly. His mother notices the colorful butterfly.
5. Do you want to stay? Do you want to go?

 QUICK WRITE Write five sentences. In each sentence, draw one line under the complete subject and two lines under the complete predicate. Then write *S* above the simple subject and *P* above the simple predicate.

Grammar

RULE 1

Nouns

- A **noun** is a word that names a person, place, thing, or idea.

  The festival was held on Monday.

RULE 2

Combining Sentences: Nouns

- Sentences with related information about two different nouns may be combined by using the **conjunction** *and* or *or* to join the nouns.

  Music will be presented.   *Dance will be presented.*

  Music and dance will be presented.

Practice Combine the nouns in each sentence by using *and* or *or* to create one sentence. Underline each noun, and write whether it names a person, place, thing, or idea.

1. Many girls performed dances. Many boys performed dances.

2. The stage in our school had lights. The stage had props.

RULE 3

Singular and Plural Nouns

- A **singular noun** names one person, place, thing, or idea.
- A **plural noun** names more than one person, place, thing, or idea.
- Most plural nouns are formed by adding *-s* or *-es*.

Singular	Plural	Singular	Plural
vegetable	vegetables	sandwich	sandwiches
valley	valleys	pastry	pastries
knife	knives	woman	women

Practice Write each sentence. Draw one line under singular nouns and two lines under plural nouns.

1. Sandwiches were sold at booths next to the sidewalk.

2. The woman tasted a dish made with noodles.

RULE 4

Common and Proper Nouns

- A **common noun** names a person, place, thing, or idea.
- A **proper noun** names a particular person, place, thing, or idea and begins with a capital letter.

Practice Write each sentence. Draw one line under each common noun and two lines under each proper noun.

1. The women admired the costumes from India.

2. A Native American wore moccasins of leather and beads.

3. The fabrics from Africa have bold colors.

 RULE 5

Possessive Nouns

- A **possessive noun** is a noun that shows who or what owns or has something.

Description	Examples	
A singular possessive adds *'s* to a singular noun.	*horse's tail*	*fox's tracks*
	leaf's color	*child's toy*
A plural possessive adds *'* to a noun that ends with an *s* and *'s* to plural nouns that do not end with an *s*.	*two horses' tails*	*many foxes' tracks*
	many leaves' colors	*two children's toys*

Practice Write each sentence. Use the correct possessive form of the words in parentheses ( ).

1. I admired the (saddle of the Arabian horse).

2. The (daughter of the woman) clapped her hands.

3. The (tricks of the clowns) made everyone laugh.

4. The (floats of the parade) were very colorful.

5. The (weather of the day) was perfect for a parade.

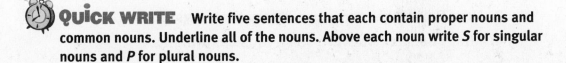 **QUICK WRITE** Write five sentences that each contain proper nouns and common nouns. Underline all of the nouns. Above each noun write *S* for singular nouns and *P* for plural nouns.

Verbs

RULE 1 — Action Verbs and Direct Objects

- An action verb is a word that tells the action of the subject.

  I wrote a story.

- A direct object is a noun or pronoun that tells to *what* or *whom* the action is done.

  She read the story.

Practice Write each sentence. Underline and write *AV* above the action verb. Underline and write *DO* above the direct object.

1. My story told an adventure.
2. I needed some paper.
3. My sister borrows my pencils.
4. I bought a notebook.
5. I finished my story.

RULE 2 — Verb Tenses

- The tense of a verb tells when something happens.

Description	Examples	
A present-tense verb shows something is happening now.	*dances*	*carries*
A past-tense verb shows something has already happened.	*danced*	*carried*
A future-tense verb shows something is going to happen.	*will dance*	*will carry*

Practice Rewrite each sentence using the correct tense of the verb in parentheses ( ).

1. Tomorrow we (watch) a play.
2. Yesterday the actors (perform) a comedy.
3. Now Rene (like) comedies better than mysteries.
4. Mrs. Thomas (want) to see a musical tonight.
5. Last year she (act) in a drama.

RULE 3

Spelling Present- and Past-Tense Verbs

- The spellings of some verbs change when *-es* or *-ed* is added.

Rules for verbs ending in:	Examples
consonant + *y* : change the *y* to *i* and add *-es* or *-ed*.	*Mavis tries to help Mom.* *Mavis tried to help Mom.*
one vowel and one consonant: double the final consonant before adding *-ed*.	*Rylie mopped the floor.*
e: drop the *e* before adding *-ed*.	*Harrison baked a cake.*

Practice Write each sentence. Use the past-tense form of the verb in parentheses ( ).

1. My classmates and I (hope) everyone would like the show.

2. The girls (skip) to the music.

3. The audience (copy) our motions.

RULE 4

Subject-Verb Agreement

- A singular verb is used with a singular subject.

  Sue wants to find a book.

- A plural verb is used with a plural subject.

  The customers want the new bestseller.

- Add *-s* to most verbs if the subject is singular and present tense.

- Do not add *-s* to the verb if the subject is plural or if the pronouns are *I* or *you*.

Practice Rewrite each sentence using the correct form of the verb in parentheses ( ).

1. The bookstore (sell, sells) hundreds of books.

2. My friends (want, wants) a book of poetry.

3. Pam and Bob (look, looks) for the comic books.

 QUICK WRITE Write five sentences that each contain an action verb. Underline the verb. Then write if the verb is in the past, present, or future tense.

Grammar

Grammar

RULE 5 — Main Verbs and Helping Verbs

- The **main verb** in a sentence shows what the subject does or is.

    The horse is **leaping** *over the fence.*

- A **helping verb** helps the main verb show an action or make a statement.

    The horse **is** *leaping over the fence.*

- Use a form of the verb *be* with the present participle.
- Use a form of the verb *have* with the past participle.

Practice: Write each sentence. Complete the sentence with a helping verb.

1. I _____ waiting for the race to begin soon.

2. The horses _____ meeting at the starting line.

3. The winner _____ finished in the fastest time.

RULE 6 — Linking Verbs

- A **linking verb** links the subject of the sentence to a noun or an adjective in the predicate. Linking verbs do not show action.

    Patricia **was** *a coach.*

- *Coach* is a noun that renames the subject.

    The gymnast **is** *strong.*

- *Strong* is an adjective that describes the subject.

Practice Complete each sentence with the linking verb in parentheses ( ). Draw one line under the noun that renames the subject. Draw two lines under the adjective that describes the subject.

1. The student _____ a champion. (be)

2. Her coach _____ skillful. (be)

3. His parents _____ supportive. (be)

4. James _____ excited. (look)

5. The team _____ ready to compete. (seem)

146

RULE 7 — Irregular Verbs

- An **irregular verb** is a verb that does not add *-d* or *-ed* to form the past tense or the past participle.
- The **helping verbs** *has, have,* and *had* are used with the past participles of irregular verbs to form other tenses.

Description	Examples
Present Tense	*Sarah runs to the park.* *She buys new shoes.*
Past Tense	*Sarah ran to the park.* *She bought new shoes.*
Past Participle	*She has run to the park before.* *She already has bought new shoes.*

Practice: Rewrite each sentence using the correct form of the verb in parentheses ( ).

1. Last night we (choose) the path around the lake.
2. Several geese had (fly) above us.
3. We (go) slowly around the path that night.
4. I have (ride) my bike here before.
5. Dan (bring) bottles of water last night.
6. He had (give) a bottle to each of us.
7. Later Sarah (throw) a stone across the water.
8. Afterwards I (drink) the rest of my water.
9. That evening, we (see) the sun go down.
10. I have never (see) a more beautiful sight.

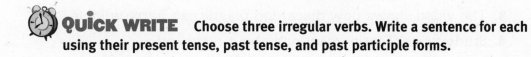

QUICK WRITE Choose three irregular verbs. Write a sentence for each using their present tense, past tense, and past participle forms.

Grammar

Grammar

RULE 1

Pronouns

- A **pronoun** is a word that takes the place of one or more nouns. A pronoun must match the noun that it replaces.

Singular Pronouns	*I, you, he, she, it, me, him, her*
Plural Pronouns	*we, you, they, us, them*

Practice Write each sentence. Replace each underlined word or words with a pronoun. Make sure that the pronoun matches the noun to which it refers.

1. <u>Maddie and Claire</u> decide to attend the meeting.

2. <u>The meeting</u> is about recycling and conservation.

3. Mr. Alden gives <u>the girls</u> permission to attend the meeting.

RULE 2

Subject Pronouns and Object Pronouns

- A **subject pronoun** can take the place of a noun that is the subject of a sentence. I, you, he, she, it, we, and they are subject pronouns.

   Mario runs the meeting.   He runs the meeting.

- An **object pronoun** can be used as the object of an action verb or after words such as *to, for, with, in,* or *at*. The words me, you, him, her, it, us, and them are object pronouns.

   Mario tells us how to protect the environment.

Practice Write each sentence. Replace the underlined noun or nouns with the correct subject or object pronoun. Underline each subject pronoun.

1. <u>Mario</u> presents information about recycling.

2. Mario asks <u>Claire and me</u> to help set up a video.

3. <u>The video</u> shows how discarded plastic can harm wildlife.

4. Students ask <u>Mario</u> questions about recycling.

5. Mario tells <u>the students</u> how to conserve natural resources.

RULE 3

Pronoun-Verb Agreement

- Subject pronouns and verbs must agree. Singular subjects go with singular verbs. Plural subjects go with plural verbs.
- Add *-s* to most verbs when you use *he, she*, or *it*. Do not add *-s* to a present-tense verb when the subject is *I, you*, or a plural pronoun.

  She asks questions.   *They ask questions.*

- A compound subject can have two pronouns with the same predicate. The verb agrees with the plural subject.

  She and I ask questions.

Practice Rewrite each sentence with the correct present-tense form of the verb in parentheses ( ).

1. He _____ the principal about our meeting. (tell)

2. He and I _____ the principal to start a recycling program. (convince)

3. She _____ that our school can help the environment. (know)

RULE 4

Possessive Pronouns

- A possessive pronoun shows *who* or *what* owns something.

  Mario's poster has information.   *His poster has information.*

- *My, your, his, her, its, our, your*, and *their* are possessive pronouns that come before nouns. *Mine, yours, his, hers, its, ours, yours*, and *theirs* are possessive pronouns that can stand alone.

  I liked your poster.   *That poster is ours.*

Practice Write each sentence. Replace the underlined word or words with the correct possessive pronoun.

1. The program succeeds due to <u>the students'</u> hard work.

2. Mr. Alden is <u>the program's</u> faculty advisor.

3. <u>Mario's</u> poster convinces others to recycle.

 QUICK WRITE   Write five sentences that include subject and object pronouns. Make sure each subject pronoun agrees with its verb.

Grammar

Grammar

RULE 1

Adjectives and Articles

- **Adjectives** are words that describe nouns or pronouns. Adjectives tell *what kind* or *how many*.

    Mount St. Helens had a violent *eruption in 1980.* *(what kind)*

    Before 1980, the volcano had few *eruptions.* *(how many)*

- *A*, *an*, and *the* are special adjectives called articles. Use *a* or *an* to refer to any one item in a group. Use *the* to refer to a specific item or more than one item.

    an eruption   *a volcano*   *the lava*

Practice **Write each sentence. Complete each sentence with an article or another adjective.**

1. Mount St. Helens is part of _____ Cascade Range.

2. _____ volcanoes are inactive and cause no harm.

3. Some volcanic eruptions have caused _____ damage.

RULE 2

Demonstrative Adjectives

- A **demonstrative adjective** tells which one or which ones.

- **This** and **these** are demonstrative adjectives that refer to something nearby.

    According to these *records,* this *volcano erupts often.*

- **That** and **those** are demonstrative adjectives that refer to something farther away.

    Look in the distance at that *volcano among* those *hills.*

Practice **Write each sentence. Complete each sentence with *this*, *that*, *these*, or *those*.**

1. Can I see _____ brochures in your hand?

2. _____ brochure has more information than this one.

3. _____ facts about volcanoes are amazing!

Grammar

RULE 3 — Comparative and Superlative Adjectives

- Use **comparative adjectives** to compare two nouns or pronouns.

    taller than   *more active than*   *better than*

- Use **superlative adjectives** to compare more than two nouns or pronouns.

    tallest of all   *most active of all*   *best of all*

Practice Write each sentence. Use the correct adjective from the pair in parentheses ( ).

1. The volcano was (large, larger) than Kayla expected.

2. It was the (more amazing, most amazing) sight she had ever seen.

3. It was the site of the (worse, worst) natural disaster in 100 years.

RULE 4 — Combining Sentences with Adjectives

- **Two sentences** that tell about the same noun can be combined by adding an adjective to one of the sentences.

    There was hot lava. The lava was black.

    There was hot, black lava.

Practice Combine each pair of sentences by adding an adjective to one of the sentences. Write the new sentence.

1. Kayla showed us pictures. There were several pictures.

2. She told about the volcano. The volcano was impressive.

3. It was a big volcano. The volcano was inactive.

 QUICK WRITE Write five sentences about your classroom. Use adjectives to describe and compare objects in the room. Include demonstrative, comparative, and superlative adjectives.

Grammar

RULE 1

Adverbs

- An **adverb** tells more about a verb. An adverb tells **how**, **when**, or **where** an action takes place.

  Theresa jogs slowly. (how)

  The race begins soon. (when)

  The fans gather nearby. (where)

- Many adverbs end in *-ly*.

  carefully   sweetly   happily   softly

Practice Write each sentence. Draw one line under the adverb. Write whether the underlined adverb tells *how*, *when*, or *where* the action takes place.

1. One runner lifted her knees high to stretch her legs.
2. Another runner sat down and stretched.
3. Theresa walked around to keep her legs limber.
4. Sometimes Theresa hopped on one foot or the other.
5. Anna hummed quietly while she waited for the race to begin.

RULE 2

Adverbs Before Adjectives and Adverbs

- **Adverbs** can describe adjectives as well as verbs.

  Theresa felt awfully nervous.

- **Adverbs** can also tell more about other adverbs.

  Her heart was beating very quickly.

Practice Write each sentence. Write whether the underlined adverb describes an adjective or another adverb.

1. Theresa was <u>extremely</u> nervous about the race.
2. She was <u>too</u> excited to notice the cheering crowd.
3. She bolted <u>very</u> quickly at the sound of the whistle.
4. She ran <u>quite</u> well during the race.
5. Theresa was <u>rather</u> happy with her progress.

RULE 3

Comparing with Adverbs

- **Adverbs** can compare two or more actions.

To Compare Two Actions

Add *-er* to most short adverbs.	*longer, higher, slower*
Use *more* with an adverb that has two or more syllables.	*more quietly, more patiently*

To Compare Three or More Actions

Add *-est* to most short adverbs.	*longest, highest, slowest*
Use *most* with an adverb that has two or more syllables.	*most quietly, most patiently*

Practice Write each sentence. Choose the correct comparative or superlative adverb from the parentheses ( ).

1. Theresa ran (more quickly, most quickly) than the others.

2. Theresa had trained (harder, more hard) than her competitors.

3. Of all the fifth-graders, Theresa ran (more swiftly, most swiftly).

RULE 4

Negatives

- A **negative** is a word that means "no." Do not use a **double negative** in one sentence. Correct a double negative by changing one negative into a positive word.

  She didn't want anyone to feel bad about the race.

Practice Write each sentence correctly, using only one negative.

1. Before long, there wasn't no one left on the track.

2. After the race, Theresa didn't have no energy to celebrate.

3. Theresa didn't want to do nothing but sleep.

 QUICK WRITE Write six sentences with adverbs. Include a least one comparative adverb and one superlative adverb. Also include at least one negative.

153

Grammar

RULE 1

Interjections

- An **interjection** is a word or group of words that expresses strong feeling.

    Oops! We forgot to put film in the camera.

- A **comma** is used after a mild interjection.

    Gee, I guess we should have checked the camera.

- An **exclamation mark** is used after an interjection that expresses very strong feeling.

    Hey! Maybe there is film in our backpacks.

Practice **Rewrite each sentence using correct capitalization and punctuation.**

1. Look there is film in my backpack

2. Hooray we will have pictures to remember our trip

3. Well should we start on our hike

4. Oh no the flash doesn't seem to be working

5. Yikes we forgot to replace the batteries

RULE 2

Prepositions

- A **preposition** is a word that relates a noun or pronoun to another word in a sentence.

    My family enjoys traveling during the summer.

Common Prepositions

about	among	beside	from	off	to
above	around	between	in	on	under
across	at	by	inside	out	until
after	before	down	into	outside	up
against	behind	during	near	over	with
along	below	for	of	through	without

Practice Write each sentence. Choose a preposition to complete the sentence.

1. Our family enjoys spending time _____ each other.

2. We drive _____ the mountains.

3. We hike _____ the trails.

4. The trails curve _____ the river.

5. The view _____ the mountains is beautiful.

RULE 3

Prepositional Phrases

- A prepositional phrase begins with a preposition and ends with a noun or pronoun.

   We love to explore near the river.

- The object of a preposition is the noun or pronoun that follows the preposition.

   There is a bridge over the river.

- When the object of a preposition is a pronoun, use an object pronoun, such as *me, you, him, her, it, us*, or *them*.

   You can see over it to the other side.

Practice Write each sentence. Draw one line under the prepositional phrase. Draw two lines under the object of the preposition.

1. My brother walked across the bridge.

2. He looked at the clear, blue water.

3. My parents brought a picnic for us.

4. After lunch, we spread out a blanket and relaxed.

5. Everyone rested under a large, shady tree.

 QUICK WRITE Write five sentences with interjections and prepositional phrases. Underline each prepositional phrase, and circle the object of the preposition.

Titles and Names

- An **abbreviation** is a shortened form of a word. An **initial** is the first letter of a name. Titles and initials begin with a capital letter and end with a period.

Title	Abbreviation	Title	Abbreviation
men	Mr.	Doctor	Dr.
women	Ms.	Senator	Sen.
married women	Mrs.	Governor	Gov.

Name	Initials
John Robert	J. R.
Nancy Jane	N. J.

Organizations

- In both formal and informal writing, use abbreviations for certain organizations and government agencies. These abbreviations usually have all capital letters and no periods.

  United Nations   UN   Federal Bureau of Investigations   FBI

Internet Addresses

- Use abbreviations at the end of Internet addresses.

commercial	.com	educational	.edu
organization	.org	network	.net

Practice Rewrite each sentence. Change each word or group of words in parentheses ( ) to an abbreviation or initials.

1. Our class contacted the (Department of Natural Resources).

2. We talked to a man named (Doctor) (Paul James) Donahue.

3. We asked about (woman) Keller, a famous botanist.

4. Our class was told to contact her at www.geese. (organization).

5. (woman) Keller works for the (Environmental Protection Agency).

Time

- Use abbreviations to indicate time before noon and after noon. These abbreviations are capitalized with periods after each letter.

Abbreviation	Meaning
11:00 A.M.	11:00 ante meridiem (before noon)
11:00 P.M.	11:00 post meridiem (after noon)

Days and Months

- In informal writing, use abbreviations of the days of the week and the months of the year. These abbreviations begin with a capital letter and end with a period.

Day	Abbreviation	Month	Abbreviation
Monday	Mon.	January	Jan.
Tuesday	Tues.	February	Feb.
Wednesday	Wed.	March	Mar.
Thursday	Thurs.	April	Apr.
Friday	Fri.	May	May
Saturday	Sat.	June	June
Sunday	Sun.	July	July
		August	Aug.
		September	Sept.
		October	Oct.
		November	Nov.
		December	Dec.

Addresses

- Address abbreviations are capitalized and followed by a period.

Avenue	Ave.	Drive	Dr.
Street	St.	Road	Rd.
Boulevard	Blvd.	Post Office	P.O.

Grammar

Grammar

States

- **United States Postal Service** abbreviations for the names of states consist of two capital letters. No period follows these abbreviations.

State	Abbreviation	State	Abbreviation
Alabama	AL	Montana	MT
Alaska	AK	Nebraska	NE
Arizona	AZ	Nevada	NV
Arkansas	AR	New Hampshire	NH
California	CA	New Jersey	NJ
Colorado	CO	New Mexico	NM
Connecticut	CT	New York	NY
Delaware	DE	North Carolina	NC
Florida	FL	North Dakota	ND
Georgia	GA	Ohio	OH
Hawaii	HI	Oklahoma	OK
Idaho	ID	Oregon	OR
Illinois	IL	Pennsylvania	PA
Indiana	IN	Rhode Island	RI
Iowa	IA	South Carolina	SC
Kansas	KS	South Dakota	SD
Kentucky	KY	Tennessee	TN
Louisiana	LA	Texas	TX
Maine	ME	Utah	UT
Maryland	MD	Vermont	VT
Massachusetts	MA	Virginia	VA
Michigan	MI	Washington	WA
Minnesota	MN	West Virginia	WV
Mississippi	MS	Wisconsin	WI
Missouri	MO	Wyoming	WY

Units of Measure

- Use abbreviations for units of measure. The abbreviation is the same for singular and plural units.

in.—inch(es)   lb.—pound(s)   km—Kilometer(s)   L—liter(s)

Grammar

First Words

- Capitalize the first word of a sentence.

  My sister is going to camp.

- Capitalize the first word of a direct quotation. Do not capitalize the second part of an interrupted quotation.

  Dan cried, "Please stop the presses!"
  "I am leaving," Jan declared, "as soon as I can."

- When the second part of a quotation is a new sentence, put a period after the interrupting expression and capitalize the first word of the new sentence.

  "I know that song," said Lisa. "We learned it last week."

- Capitalize all words in the greeting of a letter.

  Dear Sirs: *Dear Friend,*

- Capitalize the first word in the closing of a letter.

  Sincerely,   *Yours truly,*

- Capitalize the first word of each line of poetry unless the word is not capitalized in the original piece.

  I shot an arrow into the air,
  It fell to earth, I know not where;
  For, so swiftly it flew, the sight
  Could not follow it in its flight.

Practice Rewrite the friendly letter correctly. Use capital letters where needed.

(1) dear friend,

(2) how are you? Let me just say, **(3)** "here is a poem for you."

(4) roses are red.

Violets are blue.

Sugar is sweet.

And so are you.

                              (5) your friend,

                              Michael

Grammar

Proper Nouns: Names and Titles of People

- Capitalize the names of people and the initials that stand for their names.

  James Robert Perry   *J. R. Perry*

- Capitalize titles or abbreviations of titles when they come before or after the names of people.

  Mr. James Perry, Jr.   General J. P. Perry   Dr. Ellen Mahoney

- Capitalize words that show family relationships when used as titles or as substitutes for a person's name.

  Then Dad and Grandma Ellen cooked dinner.

- Do not capitalize words that show family relationships when they are preceded by a possessive noun or pronoun.

  Diane's grandmother is a good cook. Her dad is a good cook, too.

- Capitalize the pronoun *I*.

  Can I help cook dinner?

Practice Rewrite each sentence correctly. Capitalize the names and titles of people where needed.

1. p. j. and i made brownies for the family party.
2. My uncle, general steven ross, loved them.
3. My uncle and i ate five brownies each.
4. Father helped grandpa make pasta.
5. Grandpa said that mr. matthews gave him the recipe.

160

Proper Nouns: Names of Places

- Capitalize the names of cities, states, countries, and continents. Do not capitalize articles or prepositions that are part of the name.

City	*Austin*
State	*Texas*
Country	*United States of America*
Continent	*North America*

- Capitalize the names of bodies of water and geographical features.

  Atlantic Ocean   *Niagara Falls*

- Capitalize the names of sections of the country.

  the South   *the Pacific Northwest*

- Do not capitalize compass points when they just show direction.

  New York is east of Cleveland.

- Capitalize the names of streets and highways.

  Elm Street   *Santa Ana Freeway*

- Capitalize the names of buildings, bridges, and monuments.

  Sears Tower   *Brooklyn Bridge*   *Jefferson Memorial*

- Capitalize the names of stars and planets.

  The closest star to our planet is Proxima Centauri.

  The planet closest to the sun is Mercury.

- Capitalize *Earth* when it refers to the planet. Do not capitalize *earth* when preceded by *the*. Do not capitalize *sun* or *moon*.

  One moon revolves around Earth.

  The earth revolves around the sun.

Practice **Rewrite each sentence correctly. Use capital letters where needed.**

1. Our class drove through titusville, florida, to visit the john f. kennedy space center.

2. The bus drove south along cheney highway.

3. We looked at the atlantic ocean, and then we went inside to learn about space.

4. We learned about the crab nebula, an exploding star far from earth.

5. We also learned about mars, the fourth planet from the sun.

Grammar

Other Proper Nouns and Adjectives

- Capitalize the names of schools, clubs, businesses, and political parties.

  Albright Middle School   *Explorers' Club*

  Reynold's Pharmacy   *Democratic Party*

- Capitalize the names of historic events, periods of time, and documents.

  Battle of Bunker Hill   *Colonial Period*

  Declaration of Independence

- Capitalize the days of the week, months of the year, and holidays. Do not capitalize the names of the seasons.

  We started school on Tuesday, September 1.

  Our first vacation is on Labor Day.

  My favorite season is autumn.

- Capitalize abbreviations.

  Dr.   *Ave.*   *Sept.*   *Ln.*

- Capitalize the names of ethnic groups, nationalities, and languages.

  The French won the war.   *I speak Japanese.*

- Capitalize proper adjectives that are formed from the names of ethnic groups and nationalities.

  Italian bread   *Egyptian cotton*

- Capitalize the first word of each main topic and subtopic in an outline.

  I.   *Products and exports*

     A.   *Natural resources*

     B.   *Manufactured goods*

Practice Rewrite each sentence correctly. Use capital letters where needed.

1. The fifth graders at jefferson elementary are studying the louisiana purchase.

2. The jeffersonville historical society has helped them gather information.

3. The Louisiana Territory had been changing hands since the seven years' war.

4. spanish, french, and british troops had all occupied the territory.

5. The students wondered if the troops spoke english.

Titles of Works

- Capitalize the first, last, and all important words in the title of a book, play, short story, poem, film, article, newspaper, magazine, TV series, chapter of a book, and song.

    I can't wait to read *Roll of Thunder, Hear My Cry*.

    Did you see *Peter Pan* at the community theater?

    A clever short story is "Rip van Winkle."

    My favorite poem when I was young was "Old King Cole."

    You should read "Cars of the Future" in this month's *Vehicles Monthly*.

    My dad reads *The Los Angeles Times* every morning.

    Did you watch *Newsbreaker* last night?

    Chapter one of that book is titled "The Long Night."

    I sang "The Star-Spangled Banner" before the big game.

Practice **Rewrite each sentence correctly. Capitalize all titles of works.**

1. Our school newspaper, *the titan times*, prints entertainment reviews.

2. One writer liked the book *stuart little*.

3. Her favorite chapter was titled "a narrow escape."

4. Another writer reviewed a play titled *the great divide*.

5. He compared it to the short story titled "opposite ends."

6. One writer reviewed the choir's performance of "somewhere over the rainbow."

7. I remember that song from the film *the wizard of oz*.

8. Next month, I'll write a review for the television series titled *karate man*.

9. The article's title will be "getting your kicks."

10. Maybe I'll write a review of my favorite magazine, *kidsports*, too.

Grammar

End Punctuation

- Use end punctuation at the end of a sentence.
- A period ends a declarative sentence. A declarative sentence makes a statement.

  I have a cold.
- A period ends an imperative sentence. An imperative sentence makes a command or a request.

  Keep yourself warm.
- A question mark ends an interrogative sentence. An interrogative sentence asks a question.

  Will I get well?
- An exclamation mark ends an exclamatory sentence. An exclamatory sentence expresses strong emotion.

  I finally feel better!

Periods

- Use a period at the end of an abbreviation (in informal writing).

  Dr.   St.   Tues.   Jan.
- Use a period in abbreviations for time (in both formal and informal writing).

  12:00 A.M.   12:00 P.M.
- Use a period after initials.

  P. J. Reynolds
- Use a period after numbers and letters in an outline.

  I. Margaret Mead
  *   A. Famous anthropologist*
  *   B. Summary of her work*

Practice Write each sentence. Use correct punctuation.

1. Do you have any chicken soup
2. At 10:00 AM, some ladies brought chicken soup to my house.
3. I liked Mrs Nelson's chicken soup best.
4. "AJ Jones," she said, "you'll feel better soon."
5. How hot it was

Grammar

Colons

- Use a colon to separate the hour and the minute when you write the time of day.

  12:45   1:15   6:30

- Use a colon after the greeting of a business letter.

  Dear Sirs: Dear Mr. Franklin:

Hyphens

- Use a hyphen or hyphens in certain compound words.

  drive-in   merry-go-round

- Use a hyphen to show the division of a word at the end of a line. Always divide the word between syllables.

  Jennifer wants to go camping and canoe-
  ing this weekend.

- Use a hyphen in compound numbers.

  twenty-two students   forty-nine stairs

Apostrophes

- Use an apostrophe and an *s* (*'s*) to form the possessive of a singular noun.

  Jason's book   my mom's bike   the car's horn

- Use an apostrophe and an *s* (*'s*) to form the possessive of a plural noun that does not end in *s*.

  children's books   men's shoes   geese's feathers

- Use an apostrophe alone to form the possessive of a plural noun that ends in *s*.

  ladies' purses   donkeys' brays   lilies' scent

- Use an apostrophe in a contraction to show where a letter or letters are missing.

  we + are = we're   he + is = he's   would + not = wouldn't

- Do not use an apostrophe in a possessive pronoun.

  its good points   their friends   your idea

Grammar

Commas

- Use a comma between the name of the city and state in an address.

  Boston, Massachusetts

- Use a comma after the name of a state or a country when it is used with the name of a city in a sentence.

  We visited San Francisco, California, on our vacation.

- Use a comma between the day and year in a date.

  April 20, 2002   *July 4, 1776*

- Use a comma before and after the year when it is used with both the month and the day in a sentence. Do not use a comma if only the month and the year are given.

  June 4, 2000, is our last day of school.

  We will begin middle school in September 2001.

- Use a comma after the greeting in a friendly letter and after the closing in all letters.

  Dear Tyler,   *Sincerely,*

Practice Rewrite the following friendly letter. Place commas where needed.

124 Higgins Street

(1) Pittsburgh PA 15212

(2) September 4 2009

(3) Dear Mariela

(4) On September 30 2009 I will be coming to town.

(5) Your friend

Grace

Commas

- Use commas to separate three or more items in a series.

  Our flag is red, white, and blue.

  You are kind, patient, and helpful.

- Use a comma before *and, but,* or *or* when it joins simple sentences to form a compound sentence.

  We like to play softball, but the field is often used.

  My mother can drive us, or we can take the bus.

Practice Rewrite each sentence correctly. Add commas where they are needed.

1. We unloaded the balls bats and catcher's equipment for the big game.

2. I hope I'll be pitcher but I'm not sure whether I'll be chosen.

3. A pitcher has to be smart fast and accurate.

4. Our games are exciting and many people cheer.

5. We score early in the game or we depend on good pitching.

Commas

- Use a comma after introductory words or phrases in a sentence.
  Yes, I enjoy science class.
- Use a comma to set off a noun of direct address.
  Greta, please pass the mustard.
- Use a comma to set off a direct quotation.
  "I'll be right there," I said.
  "Will you please," I added, "pass the salt?"
- Use a comma after an introductory prepositional phrase.
  To the right of the tree, you'll see the monument.
  Behind the house, my family is waiting.
- Use a comma to prevent misreading.
  To a tall girl like Joan, Taylor seems really short.

Practice Rewrite each sentence. Add commas where needed.

1. Mom are you ready for the family reunion?

2. Yes I'm ready.

3. Well I'm not.

4. As you know we haven't prepared anything for the potluck supper.

5. On the table you'll find the recipe for the beans.

6. Over the stove you'll find the ingredients.

7. Yes Mom I'll make the beans.

8. Like my mom I enjoy cooking.

9. "You are both great cooks" my dad said.

10. "I think" I replied "you're right!"

Grammar

Quotation Marks

- Use **quotation marks** before and after a direct quotation, the exact words that a speaker says.

  "Someday I'm going to Brazil," said Paul.

  "Someday," said Paul, "I'm going to Brazil."

- Use a **comma** or **commas** to separate a phrase, such as *he said*, from the quotation itself. Place the comma outside the opening quotation marks but inside the closing quotation marks.

  Veronica asked, "Would you like to go to China?"

  "When I get older," replied Adam, "I'd love to go there."

- Place a **period** inside closing quotation marks.

  Pam added, "I hear Singapore is beautiful, too."

- Place a **question mark** or an **exclamation mark** inside the quotation marks when it is part of the quotation.

  "Where do you want to travel?" asked Maria.

  "I want to go on safari in Kenya, of course!" shouted Lily.

- Use **quotation marks** around the title of a short story, song, short poem, magazine or newspaper article, and chapter of a book.

  "Jack and the Beanstalk"   "Yankee Doodle Dandy"

  "How Valentine's Day Came to Be"   "Little Miss Muffet"

  "Hurricane Floyd Rocks the Southeast"   "A Mysterious Visitor"

Practice Rewrite each sentence correctly. Add punctuation where needed.

1. Are you ready for Around-the-World Day asked Mrs. Lee.

2. I want to learn about Jamaica said Isabel.

3. Will we asked Kevin learn about Ireland?

4. Yes replied Mrs. Lee we will.

5. Michael exclaimed What fun this day will be!

6. Did you enjoy the story titled Best Player?

7. Yes, it reminded me of the poem Casey at the Bat.

8. It made me think of the song Take Me Out to the Ballgame.

9. I read an article titled Greatest Baseball Players in History.

10. Now I look for books with chapter titles such as Home Run Kings.

Italics (Underlining)

- Use italics or underlining to enclose the title of a book, film, television series, play, magazine, or newspaper.

The Secret Garden	The Secret Garden
Dumbo	Dumbo
Reading Rainbow	Reading Rainbow
Fiddler on the Roof	Fiddler on the Roof
Sports Illustrated	Sports Illustrated
The New York Times	The New York Times

Practice Rewrite each sentence correctly. Underline titles where needed.

1. Did you know that the movie Alice in Wonderland was based on a book?

2. Yes, the book was titled Alice's Adventures in Wonderland.

3. The author's life was described on a TV show called Great Authors.

4. Articles about the author also appeared in newspapers such as The Chicago Tribune.

5. The author's biography was written in Cricket magazine, too.

Grammar

Sentence Structure: Diagramming Guide

A **sentence diagram** shows how the words in a sentence go together. The diagram shows capitalized words but not sentence punctuation. The most important words in the sentence are put on a horizontal *base line*. The other words are written on lines connected to the base line. First, you will learn how to diagram the most important words in a sentence. Later, you will learn how to diagram the other words.

Simple Subjects and Simple Predicates

- The simple subject and the simple predicate are written on the base line of a sentence diagram. The simple subject is written on the left side of the base line, and the simple predicate is written on the right side. An up-and-down line separates the simple subject from the simple predicate.

Miners dig minerals.

| Miners | dig |

In an interrogative sentence, the simple subject often comes between the two parts of a verb phrase.

Have you seen the mine?

| you | Have seen |

In an imperative sentence, there may not be a named subject. In this case, the subject is *you*.

Watch that miner.

| (you) | Watch |

Practice Make a sentence diagram of the simple subject and the simple predicate in each sentence.

1. Minerals come from the earth.
2. Coal is formed between layers of rock.
3. Miners blast minerals out of the ground.
4. Does copper come from mines in Arizona?
5. Close that mine now.

Compound Subjects and Predicates

- A sentence with a compound subject has two or more simple subjects with the same predicate. A sentence with a compound predicate has two or more simple predicates with the same subject. The simple subjects or simple predicates are joined by *and* or *or*. In a sentence diagram, the word *and* or *or* is written on a dotted up-and-down line connecting the subjects or the predicates.

Rice and pasta provide energy for the body.

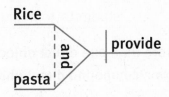

Humans work, play, and sleep.

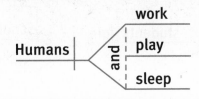

Practice Diagram the compound subject or the compound predicate in each sentence. Include in each diagram the simple subject and the simple predicate that goes with each compound.

1. Bones and teeth need calcium.

2. Some fats and oils help the body.

3. Vitamin A strengthens and improves vision.

4. Starches and sugars are carbohydrates.

5. Toddlers and women require extra iron.

6. Good food and exercise are important.

7. Oxygen and food are needed by the body.

8. A healthy body repairs and replaces damaged cells.

9. Babies, children, and teenagers need healthy food.

10. Children eat, sleep, and exercise to stay healthy.

Grammar

Grammar

 RULE 3

Direct Objects

- A direct object is a noun or pronoun in the predicate that receives the action of the verb. It answers the question *Whom?* or *What?* In a sentence diagram, the direct object is written after the simple predicate on the base line. An up-and-down line separates the direct object from the simple predicate. This vertical line does not cross the base line.

Many students join the band.

students | join | band

A verb can have more than one direct object. Look at the following example to see how a compound direct object is diagrammed.

Many students join the band, choir, or orchestra.

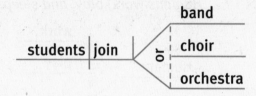

Practice Diagram the simple subject, the simple predicate, and the direct object or objects in each sentence.

1. Mrs. Jacobsen encouraged Daniel.
2. She explained the requirements.
3. Daniel joined the club.
4. The students brought costumes and props.
5. The principal planned a stage set.
6. The crew cleared the stage.
7. Some art students painted the scenery.
8. Another group designed a program.
9. Dad took photographs.
10. Mom fed the cast and crew.

Adjectives and Adverbs

- **Adjectives**, including the articles *a*, *an*, and *the*, describe nouns. Adjectives tell *what kind, which one(s)*, and *how many*. **Adverbs** describe verbs, adjectives, or other adverbs. Adverbs answer *how, when, where*, or *why*. In a sentence diagram, adjectives and adverbs are placed on slanted lines below the words they describe.

The talented drummer played loudly.

An adverb does not always appear next to the verb it describes. In the following sentence, an adverb describes another adverb.

The drummer struck the instrument very quickly.

The adverb **very** describes the adverb **quickly**. Notice how the adverbs are diagrammed.

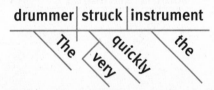

Notice how the two adjectives are diagrammed in the following example.

The bass drum boomed loudly and deeply.

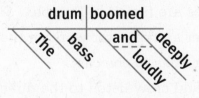

Practice Diagram every word in these sentences.

1. A single kettledrum echoes forcefully.
2. Felt covers the tenor drumsticks.
3. Ancient civilizations probably played drums.
4. Military and marching bands often play tenor drums.
5. Many famous composers wrote musical arrangements.

Grammar

Diagramming

RULE 5 — **Prepositional Phrases** —

- **Prepositional phrases** begin with a preposition such as *to, for, from, at,* or *in* and end with a noun or pronoun. In a sentence diagram, a prepositional phrase is written on a slanted line below the word that it modifies. The **object of the preposition** is written on a connecting horizontal line.

Sound and pictures are recorded separately in movies.

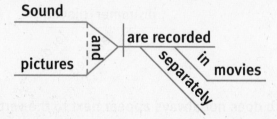

The words that describe the object of the preposition are written on slanting lines below it.

Some sounds are added to the completed film.

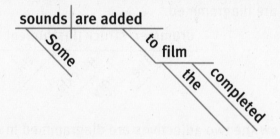

Practice **Diagram every word in these sentences.**

1. Many movies are filmed in Europe.
2. The producer and director work on the film.
3. The director talks to the cast.
4. The actors and crew listen to the director.
5. The script is written by a screenwriter.
6. Film is added to the camera.
7. The sets are created by a set designer.
8. Some costumes are repaired by the wardrobe person.
9. The music is recorded in a sound studio.
10. The movie studio pays for the movie.

Compound Sentences

- A **compound sentence** contains two or more simple sentences joined by a comma and the word *and*, *or*, or *but*. Diagram each sentence in a compound sentence separately. Write the connecting word *and*, *or*, or *but* on a line between the two sentences. Draw a dotted line connecting this word to each sentence.

Honeybees live throughout the world, but no bees live in Antarctica.

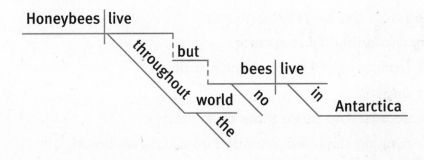

Practice Diagram every word in these compound sentences.

1. Bees are insects, and they are related to wasps.
2. A bee has two pairs of wings, but the wings are joined.
3. Pollen sticks to the bee, and it nourishes the young bees.
4. Bees sting an enemy, or they fly away.
5. Most bees attack often, but a honeybee stings only once.
6. Worker bees work, but the queen bee rules.
7. The stinger contains poison, and many people have allergic reactions to the stinger.
8. Honeycombs have rows of wax cells, and they have a pattern of holes.
9. The queen bee lays eggs, and the worker bees care for the hive.
10. Some people keep beehives, and they collect the honey.

Grammar

Extra Practice

Sentences and Sentence Fragments

A. Write *sentence* or *sentence fragment* for each group of words.

1. Our teacher is testing our fitness.

2. Long and short distances.

3. We use stopwatches to record our running time.

4. Matthew and Nashema.

5. Tired from the long-distance run.

6. I enjoy running short sprints.

7. The teacher asked us to check our pulse.

8. Our fingers.

9. We recorded our pulse rates on a chart.

10. Our running time was recorded on a bulletin board.

B. Add words to each sentence fragment to make it a complete sentence. Write the new sentence.

11. Sit-ups and push-ups.

12. Fifty sit-ups.

13. Demonstrated how to do a pull-up.

14. Held ourselves for as long as we could.

15. Had trouble doing pull-ups.

16. Practice for next year.

17. Received a ribbon.

18. The number of times.

19. My best friend.

20. Jumped rope one hundred times in a row.

C. For each pair, write the group of words that is a sentence. Then add words to the other group to make a complete thought. Write each new sentence.

21. We were tired after the tests. The students.

22. Recorded all the results. We saw our scores.

23. I need to work on pull-ups. Learned about physical fitness.

24. I will practice every day. Next year.

25. My friends and I. We will be in great shape.

Declarative and Interrogative Sentences

A. **Read each sentence. Then write whether the sentence is declarative (a statement) or interrogative (a question).**

1. Claire and I went to see a movie.

2. What movie did you see?

3. Where did you sit in the theater?

4. The movie was a mystery.

5. The main characters solved mysteries at their school.

6. One of the detectives was a young girl.

7. What were the names of the main characters?

8. Where did the movie take place?

9. The first mystery involved a missing notebook.

10. How did the detectives solve the mystery?

B. **Write each sentence. Then write whether the sentence is declarative or interrogative.**

11. My friends and I decided to find a mystery to solve.

12. Where can we find a mystery?

13. Do we know of any mysterious situations?

14. Claire had an idea.

15. We made signs to advertise our business.

16. Where should we hang the signs we made?

17. Claire's little brother brought us our first mystery.

18. Claire's brother, Jimmy, tried to find his lost toy.

19. When did he last see his toy?

20. Was anyone else playing with it?

C. **Write each sentence. Add correct punctuation.**

21. Jimmy saw the family dog near his toy

22. Where is the dog's house

23. Who wants to look inside the doghouse

24. I looked inside the doghouse and found the toy

25. Our detective agency had solved its first case

Extra Practice

Imperative and Exclamatory Sentences

A. Read each sentence. Write whether the sentence is imperative (a request or command) or exclamatory (a strong feeling).

1. Listen to the sounds in the forest.
2. How beautiful they sound!
3. Sit and close your eyes.
4. Don't make any noise.
5. What amazing noises we can hear!
6. How loud the insects are!
7. Try to hear as many different sounds as you can.
8. What a good listener you are!
9. Write the names of the noises you hear.
10. Identify as many of the sounds as you can.

B. Write each sentence. Then write whether the sentence is imperative or exclamatory.

11. Share your list of nature sounds with a friend.
12. What a complete list of sounds you made!
13. Oh, listen to that scary sound!
14. What a frightening sound that was!
15. Let's follow that noise.
16. Walk quietly along the path.
17. Listen closely.
18. How loud the noise is getting!
19. Stop, look, and listen.
20. Try to find the source of the strange sound.

C. Write each sentence. Add correct punctuation.

21. Look by that big rock
22. What an amazing sight it is
23. Take a picture of that bullfrog
24. Write about our exciting discovery
25. What a perfect ending to the day we've had

Combining Sentences: Compound Sentences

A. **Read each sentence. Write *compound* for each compound sentence. Write *simple* for each sentence that is not a compound sentence.**

1. Our class decided to clean up the school grounds.

2. The teachers agreed, and our class formed a cleanup crew.

3. We divided into teams, and each group chose a job.

4. My group collected litter.

5. We carried garbage bags, and we wore gloves on our hands.

6. I found many candy wrappers, but I didn't find any soda cans.

7. My friend Kevin was on a different cleanup team.

8. His group planted flowers, or they chose to rake leaves.

9. Students dug the holes for the flowers.

10. Kevin decided to rake, but he changed his mind.

B. **Write each sentence. Add the correct punctuation.**

11. Our cleanup group pulled weeds and we worked hard.

12. There was much work to do and we decided to work both days.

13. We chose to plant flowers the second day and I was excited.

14. I love flowers but my family doesn't plant many at our house.

15. We could plant near the school or we could plant by the park.

16. I worked near the school and I planted ten flowers.

17. The flowers were many colors but I liked the red ones best.

18. We finished planting by lunch but we had to clean our tools.

19. We could eat first or we could clean our tools first.

20. Our group was hungry but we decided to clean our tools.

C. **Combine each pair of sentences to write a compound sentence. Use a comma and the word *and, but,* or *or*.**

21. We finished our work. We were very tired.

22. The cleanup was hard work. The school looked great.

23. We took pictures of our work. We sent them to the newspaper.

24. The principal held an assembly. He thanked us for our work.

25. The school looked beautiful. We were very proud of our work.

Extra Practice

Sentence Punctuation

A. Read each sentence. Write the name of the end punctuation mark used in each sentence.

1. Our class is doing experiments with plants.

2. How many different experiments will we do?

3. Put the dirt in each of the pots.

4. Which seeds will go in each pot?

5. Please add some fertilizer to each pot.

6. How messy this experiment is!

7. There are four different plants for our experiment.

8. Each plant will grow in a different place.

9. Will you record each location on the chart?

10. Now we need to select the locations for the plants.

B. Write each sentence. Use the correct capitalization and end punctuation.

11. place the first pot by the window

12. we put the second pot in the closet

13. can we place the third pot near the chalkboard

14. where should we put the last pot

15. richard thinks the pot should be placed in the hallway

16. what a wonderful idea he had

17. please take the pot into the hall

18. let's watch the plants during the next few weeks

19. someone will need to water the plants

20. you should add "watering plants" to our job chart

C. Combine each pair of sentences to form a compound sentence. Then write each new sentence. Use the correct capitalization and punctuation.

21. it has been three weeks. we should check the plants.

22. do you want to check growth? do you want to record results?

23. the plant by the window is growing. the plant in the hall is not.

24. plants need water to grow. don't water them too much.

25. look at the growth chart. compare how much each plant grew.

Complete Subjects and Complete Predicates

A. Write the complete predicate for each sentence.

1. The students in our school present a play every year.

2. Everyone works hard to prepare for the performance.

3. The drama teacher selects the play we will perform.

4. Many students audition for a part in the play.

5. The auditions are held after school.

6. The drama teacher asks for our ideas about casting decisions.

7. The final cast list hangs on the gymnasium door.

8. All the students gather around to see the names on the list.

9. Everyone cheers for those chosen for the lead parts.

10. All students receive a role in the play.

B. Write each sentence. Draw one line under the complete subject. Draw two lines under the complete predicate.

11. Some students build the sets for the class play.

12. The sets require many hours of work.

13. The actors and actresses rehearse for several weeks.

14. The drama teacher helps students learn their lines.

15. Several parents volunteer to help make the costumes.

16. The music teacher works with students to select the music.

17. A group of students records a tape of sound effects.

18. The time for dress rehearsal arrives quickly.

19. All cast members are nervous.

20. The director sees problems at the dress rehearsal.

C. Add a complete subject or a complete predicate to each group of words. Write each new sentence.

21. Opening night

22. dressed in their costumes.

23. The audience

24. performed without a mistake.

25. Everyone in the gymnasium

Extra Practice

Simple Subjects

A. Write the simple subject in each sentence. The complete subject has been underlined to help you.

1. Our teacher suggested that each student set a personal goal.

2. The goal had to be set for a positive change.

3. Some students chose to set a goal in sports.

4. My friend wanted to score more goals in soccer.

5. Her soccer coach helped her develop a practice schedule.

6. Her teammates encouraged her to meet the goal.

7. One boy decided he would save money to buy a new bike.

8. His parents showed him how to open a bank account.

9. The money he earned was put into his account.

10. The bicycle was his in six months.

B. Write each sentence. Draw one line under the complete subject. Draw two lines under the simple subject.

11. My personal goal was to improve my spelling.

12. My teacher helped me develop a plan to meet my goal.

13. My first job was to keep a list of spelling words in my notebook.

14. The list included new words and words I had trouble spelling.

15. The spelling list was useful as I wrote stories.

16. My friends quizzed me on the school bus.

17. My father helped me practice the words during breakfast.

18. Another spelling strategy was to write the words each day.

19. Many hours were spent studying spelling words.

20. Spelling tests seem easy now.

C. Add a simple subject to each group of words. Then write the sentence.

21. thought of a personal goal.

22. gave us a goal to reach.

23. developed a plan to meet our goal.

24. kept track of our progress toward our goal.

25. were proud of the things we accomplished.

Simple Predicates

A. Write the simple predicate in each sentence. The complete predicate has been underlined to help you.

1. Thomas Jefferson studied history, architecture, and science.
2. Jefferson loved learning about nature as a boy.
3. He learned about nature in the forests by his home.
4. His sister Jane encouraged him to explore.
5. Thomas Jefferson played the violin.
6. He attended college in Williamsburg, Virginia.
7. The American colonies belonged to England at that time.
8. After college, Jefferson decided to become a lawyer.
9. He worked for five years in a friend's law office.
10. Jefferson achieved many of his goals.

B. Write each sentence. Draw one line under the simple predicate.

11. Thomas Jefferson designed the plan for his house.
12. He called his home Monticello.
13. The people of Virginia elected Jefferson to the House of Burgesses.
14. He represented the colony of Virginia.
15. Thomas Jefferson wrote the Declaration of Independence.
16. Jefferson finished the draft in two days.
17. He traveled to France to discuss the new United States.
18. Later, Jefferson served as the first Secretary of State.
19. In 1801, he became the third president.
20. Jefferson believed there were always new things to learn.

C. Add a simple predicate to each group of words. Then write the sentence.

21. Thomas Jefferson
22. The American Colonies
23. British troops
24. Some people
25. The United States

Extra Practice

Combining Sentences: Compound Subjects

A. **Write each sentence. Underline the conjunction that joins the compound subject.**

1. My aunt and uncle invite our family to their farm each year.
2. Their friends and neighbors are very nice.
3. Their son and daughter are the same age as my sister and I.
4. Chickens and ducks always come to greet us.
5. The pasture and barn are perfect places in which to play.
6. The stream and the lake are good for wading and fishing.
7. My sister and I help with work on the farm.
8. Apples and pears are ripe for picking.
9. My aunt or cousins help my uncle bale the hay.
10. My mother and father load the bales of hay onto the truck.

B. **Write each sentence. Draw one line under the compound subject.**

11. My aunt and uncle teach us how to make preserves.
12. Peaches or strawberries make the best preserves.
13. My sister and I have jobs on the farm.
14. Cows and pigs need to be fed.
15. The barn and chicken coop are cleaned every day.
16. The dog and cat are cared for every morning.
17. Roosters and ducks are noisy in the morning.
18. Crickets and frogs make noise at night.
19. Work and play make me tired on my farm visits.
20. My family and I look forward to spending time on the farm.

C. **Write each pair of sentences as one sentence with a compound subject.**

21. Horses live in the barn. Cows live in the barn.
22. The lofts are full of spiderwebs. The cellars are full of spiderwebs.
23. Apples are juicy and ripe. Pears are juicy and ripe.
24. The streams are full of fish. The lakes are full of fish.
25. Farms are interesting places. Ranches are interesting places.

Combining Sentences: Compound Predicates

A. **Write each sentence. Draw one line under the compound predicate.**

1. We select and play instruments during music class.

2. The music teacher discusses and demonstrates many choices.

3. We sit and wait for a chance to try each instrument.

4. We view and touch the stringed instruments.

5. We hold and carry the woodwind and brass instruments.

6. The students smile and laugh when they bang the drums.

7. Each student stops and thinks about which instrument to choose.

8. We question and consider which choice will be best.

9. We share and discuss our ideas.

10. Each person chooses and takes an instrument.

B. **Write the complete predicate of each sentence. Then write whether the predicate is *simple* or *compound*.**

11. The band teacher invites new members to join the group.

12. We attend practice sessions after school.

13. We learn and follow the rules of the class.

14. The teacher leads and directs each session.

15. The percussion players tap on their instruments.

16. The violinists use bows for their instruments.

17. People blow and toot the brass instruments.

18. The music teacher smiles and nods at the new players.

19. We clean and tune our instruments regularly.

20. We practice and play our instruments every day.

C. **Write each pair of sentences as one sentence with a compound predicate.**

21. The band practices together. The band plays together.

22. Our lessons begin on time. Our lessons end on time.

23. Beginning musicians practice. Beginning musicians learn.

24. The teacher directs the band. The teacher supports the band.

25. We respect our band teacher. We admire our band teacher.

Extra Practice

Correcting Run-on Sentences

A. Read each sentence. Write *run-on* for each run-on sentence. Write *correct* for each sentence that is correct.

1. My class decided to create a school newspaper.

2. Our teacher thought a newspaper was a great idea.

3. Students discussed story ideas we made a list.

4. Everyone read through the list some students had other ideas.

5. The top ten ideas were selected for further research.

6. Our teacher divided us into ten teams we began working on our lists.

7. Each team selected a topic to research and include in a report.

8. Members of one group chose sporting events they listed the top players.

9. Another team decided to write about school assemblies.

10. Members of another team chose to write about teachers they listed names.

11. The comic section was a popular choice I am not a good artist.

12. My team chose to write about current events.

13. The teacher told us we could change jobs throughout the year.

14. We thought taking turns was fair we knew waiting would be difficult.

15. The teams met to discuss how to begin they made a plan.

16. My team had four students we were all friends.

17. The team shared ideas we listed what needed to be done.

18. We needed several students to cover all the current events.

19. We decided to write two interesting news stories.

20. We knew there was much work to do we were excited.

B. Correct each run-on sentence by separating it into two sentences. Write *correct* if a sentence is correct.

21. I chose to write about the food drive my team approved.

22. Tanya wanted to write that story, but she let me do it.

23. The team members assigned me one more article that was okay with me.

24. They asked me to write a paragraph about our new school rules.

25. I thought about the information to include in my articles I wrote my ideas.

26. I wrote down a list of questions to answer.

27. The questions helped me organize my ideas I was ready to begin.

28. I finished one of my articles I needed help with the other one.

29. The principal answered questions about my second article.

30. My teammates edited my articles after I finished writing.

C. Correct each run-on sentence by separating it into two sentences or by forming a compound sentence. Write each new sentence.

31. The teacher monitored our work she helped us plan ahead.

32. We could type the articles we could write them neatly.

33. She collected the articles she organized them by topic.

34. We reviewed the pages we made some changes.

35. The teacher made copies we all received a newspaper.

36. We enjoyed reading our paper we wanted others to read it.

37. We passed out the newspapers they were gone quickly.

38. We asked readers for feedback we didn't know if anyone would respond.

39. We added a suggestion box many people sent notes.

40. The school liked our newspaper we can't wait to write more.

Extra Practice

Nouns

A. Read each sentence. Write whether each underlined noun is a person, a place, a thing, or an idea.

1. A medical <u>doctor</u> spoke to our science class.

2. She told us about the <u>body</u>.

3. The <u>heart</u> pumps blood to all parts of the body.

4. <u>Dr. Gilbert</u> let us listen to her heart through a stethoscope.

5. She told us about her work at a well-known <u>hospital</u>.

6. The hospital is in <u>Minnesota</u>.

7. This <u>clinic</u> is famous for medical research.

8. Many <u>people</u> go there to receive help.

9. Dr. Gilbert told us about performing <u>transplants</u>.

10. It takes <u>courage</u> to be a doctor.

B. Write each sentence. Draw one line under each noun.

11. We learned about the body in school.

12. Humans have more than 200 bones.

13. The skeleton helps to protect the organs.

14. Bones and muscles work together.

15. Nerves alert the body to danger.

16. Signals from the brain control the organs.

17. The senses help people adjust to their environment.

18. Lungs take in oxygen for the blood to use.

19. The blood carries nutrients throughout the body.

20. The skin is our largest organ.

C. Write the nouns in each sentence. Next to each noun, write whether it names a person, a place, a thing, or an idea.

21. The body is a complex machine.

22. Many systems work together to keep the body healthy.

23. Different doctors treat different parts of the body.

24. A cardiologist treats the heart.

25. The doctor from Minnesota is a cardiologist.

Singular and Plural Nouns

A. **Read each sentence. Write whether the underlined noun is singular or plural.**

1. A botanist is a scientist who studies <u>plants</u>.

2. The Egyptians built <u>gardens</u> to observe plants.

3. A Greek is the <u>father</u> of botany.

4. Plants have scientific <u>names</u>.

5. Some names of plants are more than 250 <u>years</u> old.

6. Plants vary from <u>country</u> to country.

7. People around the <u>world</u> use plants to treat illnesses.

8. Scientists make <u>medicines</u> from plants.

9. They are interested in plants from the <u>rain forests</u>.

10. <u>Scientists</u> believe medicines can be made from rare plants.

B. **Write each sentence. Draw one line under each singular noun. Draw two lines under each plural noun.**

11. Our neighborhood planted a garden.

12. The garden provides fresh fruits and vegetables all summer.

13. Every person works at least five hours a week.

14. Volunteers pull weeds almost every day.

15. The garden needs fertilizer often.

16. The carrots and avocadoes must be washed.

17. The neighbors enjoy the harvest.

18. Salad tastes better when the tomatoes are fresh.

19. Large, fresh peppers taste good, too.

20. The pumpkins are also big this year.

C. **Write the singular and plural nouns in each sentence. Then write the plural form of each singular noun.**

21. A peach begins as a blossom on a tree.

22. A strawberry begins as a flower, too.

23. The flowering plants make our garden look pretty.

24. The bush looks beautiful in the yard.

25. What a terrible stain blueberries can make!

Extra Practice

More Plural Nouns

A. Write each noun pair by matching the noun in the left column with its correct plural form in the right column.

1. echo		women
2. woman		moose
3. half		calves
4. tomato		news
5. mouse		halves
6. news		mice
7. foot		sopranos
8. soprano		feet
9. calf		echoes
10. moose		tomatoes

B. Write each noun. Then write its plural form.

11. loaf	**16.** goose
12. cameo	**17.** wife
13. life	**18.** piano
14. ox	**19.** tornado
15. sheep	**20.** scarf

C. Write the sentences. Complete each sentence with the correct plural form of the noun in parentheses.

21. Some local _____ and women helped repair houses. (man)

22. They painted porches and patched _____. (roof)

23. A group of _____ helped clean up the yards. (child)

24. They raked lawns and bagged _____. (leaf)

25. We cooked fish and _____ to feed the volunteers. (potato)

Common and Proper Nouns

A. **Write** *common* **if the underlined word in each sentence is a common noun. Write** *proper* **if it is a proper noun.**

1. The <u>4-H Club</u> has two clubs in our town.

2. My brother belongs to the <u>club</u> led by Mr. Morello.

3. The club cleaned up the park last <u>Tuesday</u>.

4. Two young men from the club entered the <u>Olympics</u>.

5. The <u>mayor</u> honored the club for its work at the food bank.

6. The city council named the <u>leader</u> "Man of the Year."

7. Both clubs marched in the parade along <u>Third Avenue</u>.

8. The children sang a <u>song</u> for the town meeting.

9. The performance moved the <u>audience</u> to tears.

10. The <u>organization</u> is an asset to the Huntsville area.

B. **Write each sentence. Draw one line under the common nouns and two lines under the proper nouns.**

11. The 4-H Club was founded in the United States.

12. The organization sponsors camps all across the country.

13. Many young people participate in 4-H Clubs.

14. These clubs work with county governments.

15. Their emblem is a four-leaf clover.

16. The letters represent *head*, *heart*, *hands*, and *health*.

17. The 4-H Club is supported by Congress.

18. The National 4-H Council offers many programs.

19. This council gives courses in schools.

20. Boys and girls can join in many parts of the nation.

C. **Write the nouns in each sentence. Next to each noun, write** *common* **or** *proper*. **Capitalize the proper nouns.**

21. Volunteers for 4-H clubs donate time and money.

22. Leaders often drive more than 300 miles each year.

23. Another national club is the boy scouts of america.

24. The girl scouts of america is a well-respected organization.

25. Members sell cookies to raise money.

Extra Practice

Capitalization

A. Choose the word or group of words in each pair that should be capitalized. Then write it using the correct capitalization.

1.	april	raindrop
2.	doctor	dr. bradley
3.	valentine's day	heart
4.	novel	*charlotte's web*
5.	wednesday	tomorrow
6.	brother	gary
7.	woman	mrs.
8.	"you are my sunshine"	song
9.	poem	"what is pink?"
10.	birthday	sunday

B. Write the words that should begin with capital letters. Capitalize each word correctly.

11. Our club meets every tuesday.

12. The club leader is mr. parker.

13. We begin each meeting by singing "america."

14. Sometimes we read books such as *a taste of blackberries*.

15. Other days our club watches videos such as *runaway ralph*.

16. The club attended the ballet in january.

17. For st. patrick's day, we put on a play.

18. The smith family directed the play for us.

19. Next friday our club will go on a field trip to the theater.

20. We will watch actors perform in *the pied piper*.

C. Write each sentence. Write a proper noun to replace the underlined words.

21. We don't have school on a winter holiday.

22. The club will meet on a weekday because of the holiday.

23. To celebrate, we will sing a holiday song.

24. Then we will read a holiday story.

25. That holiday makes the month my favorite time of year.

Possessive Nouns

A. Write the possessive form of each noun.

1. Rosa
2. painter
3. computer
4. Springfield
5. president
6. uncle
7. dog
8. city
9. Mrs. Stein
10. nurse

11. scientists
12. orchestras
13. children
14. tuxedos
15. calendars
16. relatives
17. counties
18. women
19. musicians
20. sponsors

B. Write each sentence. Rewrite the words in parentheses to include a plural possessive noun.

21. (The instruments of the musicians) were tuned, polished, and ready to be played.
22. (The performance of the players) was outstanding.
23. (The chairs of the spectators) were very comfortable.
24. (The help of the ushers) was appreciated by all the people in the audience.
25. (The solos of the students) received standing ovations.
26. Everyone enjoyed (the choir of children).
27. The program included (the names of the composers) and information about their lives.
28. (The seats of the balconies) were full.
29. (The batons of the conductors) looked like blurry lines.
30. (The families of the musicians) were proud of the students and their performance.

Combining Sentences: Nouns

A. **Write the two nouns that are joined by a conjunction in each sentence. Include the conjunction in your answer.**

1. Trees need good soil and water.

2. Trees and grass make their own food.

3. Bacteria and fungi cause decay.

4. Lakes provide food and shelter for animals.

5. Plants need light and water to grow.

6. Birds and butterflies migrate south for the winter.

7. Trees and flowers produce seeds.

8. People eat berries and nuts from trees.

9. Aspen trees and spruce trees grow in Colorado.

10. Rain and snow can cause flooding.

B. **Write the two nouns you can join to combine each pair of sentences.**

11. You can plant a tree. You can plant a garden.

12. Boys are cleaning up the beach. Girls are cleaning up the beach.

13. Glass can be recycled. Cans can be recycled.

14. Gardens make a community beautiful. Parks make a community beautiful.

15. I feed the birds in the winter. I feed the deer in the winter.

16. Some people live in cities. Some people live in towns.

17. We grow our own peaches. We grow our own tomatoes.

18. Schools can recycle paper. Businesses can recycle paper.

19. They reuse bottles. They reuse cartons.

20. Miguel joined the Sierra Club. Jon joined the Sierra Club.

C. **Rewrite each pair of sentences by combining two nouns.**

21. The club will recycle. The team will recycle.

22. Birds need clean water. Fish need clean water.

23. Pollution harms people. Pollution harms animals.

24. Shrubs need light. Shrubs need water.

25. People need food. People need shelter.

Letter Punctuation

A. Write the following words and phrases from business letters. Correct the five examples that contain errors in capitalization and punctuation.

1. Sincerely,
2. May 4, 2001
3. Dear Mrs. Johnson,
4. Yours truly,
5. Orlando Florida

6. Best wishes
7. respectfully,
8. Detroit, Michigan
9. Dear Ms. Torres:
10. September, 21 2002

B. Write the following phrases from business letters. Correct each mistake in capitalization and punctuation.

11. Yours truly
12. April 3 2001
13. Dear Governor Thompson
14. Phoenix Arizona
15. respectfully yours,

16. November 17 2002,
17. Dear Mr. Adolphus,
18. Baltimore Maryland,
19. best Wishes,
20. August, 23 2002

C. Write each numbered item or sentence in the following letter. Add the correct punctuation mark where needed.

21. 770 Chicago St
    Bronson, Michigan 49028
22. September 5 2000

Mrs. June Taylor
Bronson Floral Company
63 Douglas Avenue
23. Bronson Michigan 49028
24. dear Mrs. Taylor

The fifth-grade civics committee is visiting Fair Lawn Senior Home next month. We would like to give residents small bouquets. We are hoping you can help with a donation of flowers.

I believe your donations will bring smiles to many faces and will give you a way to dispose of old flowers. I will be calling soon to see if you can help. Thank you.

25. Sincerely
    Kenny Jones
    Kenny Jones

Extra Practice

Action Verbs

A. **Write the action verb in each sentence.**

1. Our family drove to the state fair.

2. Jamie watched the rodeo.

3. Andrew ate two corn dogs.

4. Jenna rode the merry-go-round.

5. My mother sewed a quilt for the quilt show.

6. The quilt won a blue ribbon.

7. Our family played carnival games.

8. My dad threw basketballs.

9. Jamie pitched pennies.

10. We stayed until after dark.

B. **Write each sentence. Replace each underlined action verb with a different action verb.**

11. A little girl rode a gray pony.

12. A clown made funny faces.

13. Artists carved statues.

14. People toured the exhibits.

15. I chose cotton candy for a snack.

16. Firefighters demonstrated safety techniques.

17. The crowd loved the parade.

18. My family watched a concert.

19. The musicians sang country songs.

20. We rode home after midnight.

C. **Write each sentence. Complete each sentence with an action verb.**

21. I _____ my little sister in a wagon.

22. My brother _____ a backpack full of prizes.

23. My parents _____ us every year.

24. We _____ a lot of treats.

25. Everyone _____ the fair.

Direct Objects

A. **Write the direct object in each sentence.**

1. These pets perform tricks.

2. The collie fetches the ball.

3. The kitten climbs a rope.

4. A parakeet rings a bell.

5. A monkey rides a tricycle.

6. Two mice run a race.

7. The gerbil spins the wheel.

8. A retriever catches a ball.

9. The beagle climbs a ladder.

10. The animals eat their treats.

B. **Write the sentences. Choose a direct object to complete each sentence.**

11. The dog owners entered a _____.

12. The shepherd wears a _____.

13. The labrador fetches some _____.

14. The beagle digs a _____.

15. A girl called her _____.

16. A boy commanded his _____.

17. A woman washed her _____.

18. A poodle circled a _____.

19. The judge blew a _____.

20. The winner received a _____.

C. **Use each word as the direct object in a sentence. Write each new sentence.**

21. beagle

22. brush

23. trophy

24. collar

25. ball

Extra Practice

Verb Tenses

A. Write *present*, *past*, or *future* to name the tense of the underlined verb.

1. Tomorrow we <u>will explore</u> the forest.
2. Curtis <u>finds</u> the trail.
3. Carrie <u>packs</u> carefully for the trip.
4. I <u>packed</u> my flashlight and compass.
5. We <u>will hike</u> most of the day.
6. Curtis <u>climbs</u> very quickly.
7. Carrie <u>asked</u> me to hold her pack.
8. I <u>examine</u> the wildflowers in the field.
9. The flowers <u>will bloom</u> soon.
10. The sun <u>shone</u> brightly.

B. Write each sentence. Complete each sentence with the correct tense of the verb in parentheses.

11. Yesterday I (see) a woodpecker in a tree.
12. Now an eagle (fly) overhead.
13. Soon we (walk) carefully around the boulder.
14. At this time of day, the tree (provide) shade.
15. Two hours ago we (eat) our lunch under a pine tree.
16. Curtis (clean) up now.
17. Tomorrow Carrie (lead) the way through the forest.
18. Last night I (find) a pinecone.
19. Tonight we (stay) at a campsite.
20. All of us (enjoy) ourselves on our last trip.

C. Write the sentences. Underline each verb. Write *present*, *past*, or *future* to describe the tense of the verb you underlined.

21. Tomorrow we will explore the lakeshore.
22. I saw many birds there last year.
23. Curtis wants to go this time.
24. Last night Carrie asked her cousin about hiking trails.
25. Now everyone packs his or her own supplies.

Subject-Verb Agreement

A. Write *singular* or *plural* to show if the underlined subject and verb in each sentence are in the singular or plural form.

1. Julie enjoys plays.

2. Tim likes the stage.

3. They write plays together.

4. Amelia watches the people around her.

5. The people give her ideas for plays.

6. Tim reads Amelia's work.

7. Julie and Amelia give Tim some ideas.

8. Tim makes suggestions for changes.

9. His suggestions help them improve their writing.

10. They work together.

B. **Write each sentence. Use the correct form of the verb.**

11. Our drama teacher (ask, asks) us to put on a play.

12. Owen (choose, chooses) a play about a Viking ship.

13. He (enjoy, enjoys) sailing as a hobby.

14. Chris and Scott (read, reads) the narration.

15. The theatergoers (clap, claps) after the introduction.

16. Nancy (read, reads) her lines with a lot of emotion.

17. I (recite, recites) my part with feeling, too.

18. The play (remind, reminds) me of social studies class.

19. My friends (clap, claps) for me when I finish.

20. We (enjoy, enjoys) listening to our friends.

C. **Write each sentence. Choose a word from the Word Bank.**

| write | writes | like | likes | demonstrate |
| place | places | take | takes | demonstrates |

21. I _____ plays for my mother.

22. My mother _____ the plays about our family the most.

23. She _____ photos while I perform.

24. Mother _____ the photos in frames.

25. The plays _____ that I care about my family.

Extra Practice

Spelling Present- and Past-Tense Verbs

A. Write *present* or *past* to name the tense of each verb.

1. dances
2. watched
3. tries
4. learned
5. spins
6. carried
7. sees
8. cheered
9. wishes
10. hurries

B. Write each sentence. Use the present-tense form of the verb in parentheses.

11. Paula (rush) to dance class.
12. She (slip) on the studio floor.
13. Antoine (carry) Paula across the floor.
14. The teacher (examine) her ankle.
15. She (notice) that something is wrong.
16. Paula (worry) about her injury.
17. Everyone (agree) that she is okay.
18. Paula (try) to stand up.
19. She (walk) carefully across the floor.
20. The dancers (applaud) when she is done.

C. Rewrite each sentence. Use the past-tense form of the verb in parentheses.

21. Our class (attend) a dance recital.
22. The audience (buzz) with excitement.
23. The dancers (sail) onto the stage.
24. The lights (dim) as the music began.
25. The people (clap) at the end of a solo performance.

Commas

A. **Write each sentence. Place a comma or commas where they are needed in each underlined phrase.**

1. <u>James Amy and Shelby</u> want to perform.

2. <u>James what</u> do you think about a puppet show?

3. The characters could be a <u>frog a toad and an owl</u>.

4. <u>Shelby make</u> a green-and-blue frog.

5. <u>Ricardo let's</u> paint the stage.

6. <u>Yes Amy that's</u> a good idea.

7. Can we practice <u>Saturday Sunday and Monday</u>?

8. <u>Monday Tuesday and Wednesday</u> can be the days to perform.

9. <u>Yes Shelby</u> can be there.

10. <u>Okay let's</u> get started.

B. **Write each sentence. Add a comma or commas where needed in each sentence.**

11. Mom may we borrow some paint?

12. Oh let's ask Hugh to help us.

13. We'll need socks fabric and glue for the puppets.

14. The toad will be yours to make Amy.

15. Yes I'll make the owl.

16. We will need the frog the toad and the owl by today.

17. Do you want a pair of scissors a needle and some thread?

18. Let's invite parents grandparents and friends.

19. Well Ricardo is finished.

20. The show will be today tomorrow and the next day.

C. **Write each sentence. Use a comma or commas where needed. Write *correct* if the sentence is correct.**

21. Ricardo where is your puppet?

22. We know Amy that you are ready.

23. Hugh brought cookies and juice for snacks.

24. Terry Tina and Andrew came to watch.

25. Yes they really enjoyed our performance.

Extra Practice

Main Verbs and Helping Verbs

A. **Write the main verb in each sentence. Notice that each helping verb is underlined.**

1. My family <u>will</u> attend an air show.

2. We <u>have</u> waited all year.

3. My dad <u>has</u> planned our trip.

4. The trip <u>will</u> take two hours.

5. We <u>can</u> stop for lunch at noon.

6. I <u>shall</u> talk to my friends about the show.

7. Tony <u>was</u> telling me about last year's show.

8. Many planes <u>were</u> soaring through the sky.

9. Five planes <u>were</u> flying in formation.

10. One pilot <u>could</u> perform amazing tricks.

B. **Write each sentence. Draw one line under the helping verb. Draw two lines under the main verb.**

11. The air show is starting in one hour.

12. The crowd was feeling anxious.

13. The pilots were working on their airplanes.

14. One woman was preparing her parachute.

15. A biplane can carry an extra person.

16. This person will walk on the wing.

17. Five jets will fly upside down.

18. The pilots have practiced for years.

19. The planes are flying close together.

20. The jets are making incredible turns.

C. **Write the sentences. Complete each sentence with a helping verb.**

21. My mother _____ leaving before the crowd departs.

22. Mom _____ taken the long way home.

23. We _____ hoping to attend the air show next year.

24. I _____ learn to be a pilot.

25. I _____ study hard.

Using Helping Verbs

A. Write the helping verb in each sentence.

1. Taylor is joining the science club.

2. Kazuko has asked about the meetings.

3. I have belonged to the club for a month.

4. Kazuko has suggested a field trip.

5. The club is planning a trip to the science museum.

6. We are discussing the trip.

7. The museum is featuring exhibits on sound.

8. I am looking forward to the field trip.

9. We are raising money for admission.

10. The club is going to go on Saturday.

B. Write the helping verb that completes each sentence.

11. The man (has, have) taken our tickets.

12. Vern (is, are) going to this exhibit first.

13. He (is, are) expected to learn about the ear.

14. I (am, is) observing a drawing of a sound wave.

15. Vern and Vanessa (is, are) viewing a demonstration.

16. The demonstration (has, have) shown how sound travels.

17. Two people (was, were) holding a piece of ribbon.

18. Popsicle sticks (was, were) glued across the ribbon.

19. One person (was, were) tapping the first stick.

20. The rest of the sticks (was, were) moving like a wave.

C. Write the sentences. Complete each sentence with a helping verb.

21. I _____ looking forward to my next visit.

22. Vanessa _____ attended this museum before.

23. Vern and his father _____ coming back tomorrow.

24. Vern _____ hoping to speak to a sound expert.

25. Vanessa _____ asked her parents to return with her.

Extra Practice

Linking Verbs

A. Write each sentence. Draw one line under the linking verb.

1. We are good singers.

2. Sandra's voice sounds good.

3. She is ready to reach the highest notes.

4. I am a baritone.

5. My voice is soft sometimes.

6. Our voices are harmonious.

7. Sandra seems nervous today.

8. The audience looks large.

9. A school newspaper reporter will be in the front row.

10. He appears restless.

B. Write each sentence. Choose the correct linking verb in parentheses.

11. Sandra (is, are) a good soloist.

12. She (feel, feels) confident about her ability to sing.

13. The conductor (is, are) ready to begin.

14. The crowd (grow, grows) noisy.

15. The bright lights (become, becomes) hot.

16. We (is, are) certain of our talents.

17. Singing (is, are) a hobby for me.

18. Sandra and Tamesha (is, are) professional singers.

19. The audience members (seem, seems) pleased with our efforts.

20. The reporter (look, looks) happy, too.

C. Rewrite each sentence. Use the present-tense form of the linking verb in parentheses. Then draw one line under the descriptive word that the linking verb connects to the subject.

21. The concert _____ successful. (be)

22. Sandra _____ grateful to the people in the audience. (feel)

23. All the people _____ cheerful. (seem)

24. They _____ overjoyed with our performance. (look)

25. The reporter _____ enthusiastic, too. (appear)

Irregular Verbs

A. **Write the past-tense verb in each sentence.**

1. My friends and I went to a cooking class.

2. We made cookies during our first class.

3. We ate on the way.

4. Evan's mother drove us to class.

5. The teacher began the class on time.

6. We wrote recipes on note cards.

7. We brought an apron with us.

8. Carmen had two or three cookies.

9. I saw a picture of next week's recipe.

10. The cake made me hungry.

B. **Write the past tense and the past participle of these verbs.**

11. eat

12. drive

13. bring

14. ride

15. go

16. write

17. begin

18. see

19. do

20. make

C. **Write each sentence. Use the correct past-tense or past-participle form of the verb in parentheses.**

21. I (write) the recipes clearly and carefully.

22. Mother (drive) the van to pick us up.

23. Bart (ride) in the passenger seat.

24. We would have (grow) restless if we had waited any longer.

25. We should have (bring) something to read.

Extra Practice

Pronouns

A. **Write the underlined pronoun. Next to it, write _S_ if the pronoun is singular or _P_ if it is plural.**

1. Mom told <u>them</u> that today is cleaning day.

2. Kristin and Ben looked at <u>her</u> in surprise.

3. <u>She</u> pointed to the garage with a smile.

4. Ben cringed when <u>he</u> saw junk everywhere.

5. Kristin and Ben needed a plan to clean <u>it</u> up.

6. How could <u>they</u> make the job more fun?

7. "Let <u>me</u> think for a minute," Ben said.

8. "<u>I</u> have the answer," Ben shouted.

9. Kristin, <u>you</u> put on some music, and let's have a race.

10. <u>We</u> can see whose side of the garage looks cleaner.

B. **Write the sentences. Draw one line under each singular pronoun and two lines under each plural pronoun.**

11. The garage was clean, but it needed to be organized.

12. "We should store similar items together," Kristin suggested.

13. She gathered the empty boxes while Ben got a marker.

14. Ben told her to store household items separately.

15. Kristin, you can put outdoor equipment in that box.

16. Kristin and Ben whistled songs while they worked.

17. Kristin helped him lift heavy boxes.

18. He helped Kristin stack the boxes against the wall.

19. They looked at the clean, tidy garage.

20. "We make a great team," Ben said with a smile.

C. **Write each sentence. Replace each underlined word or group of words with a pronoun. Be sure the pronoun matches the noun or nouns to which it refers.**

21. <u>Kristin and Ben</u> had one more cleaning job to do.

22. Mom handed Pete, the family dog, to <u>Kristin and Ben</u>.

23. <u>Pete</u> did not want a bath, but the dog really needed one!

24. Brother and sister thought of a fun way to bathe <u>Pete</u>.

25. <u>Mom</u> laughed to see Kristin, Ben, and Pete in the sprinklers.

Subject Pronouns

A. Write the subject pronoun in each sentence.

1. We have music class every Tuesday.

2. I like our music teacher, Mrs. Rojas.

3. She plays the flute.

4. We learn how to play different musical instruments.

5. Last week, you met Mrs. Rojas' husband.

6. He is a musician with the local symphony orchestra.

7. I love to hear Mr. Rojas play the clarinet.

8. It is a wonderful instrument.

9. They sometimes play a duet for the class.

10. You wouldn't believe how sweet the music sounds!

B. Write each sentence. Underline the subject pronoun.

11. She is learning to play the tuba.

12. He is learning to play the clarinet.

13. I chose to play the trumpet.

14. We practice together each day.

15. You should hear us!

16. Every week, we meet with Mrs. Rojas.

17. She demonstrates how to play a favorite song.

18. We practice a new song every week.

19. They ask the teacher for extra help.

20. We learn to play the song beautifully.

C. Write each sentence. Replace the underlined word or words with the correct subject pronoun.

21. Patty and Jacob made their own musical instruments.

22. Patty made an instrument with a can and dried beans.

23. Jacob made an instrument with a box and rubber bands.

24. The instrument looked like a guitar.

25. Patty and I listened to Jacob play the handmade guitar.

Extra Practice

Object Pronouns

A. **Write the object pronoun in each sentence.**

1. The teacher gave us seeds to plant and test.

2. Aaron asked her for supplies for planting the seeds.

3. The teacher gave him some soil and cups.

4. Everyone used them for planting.

5. Nadia helped me plant some seeds.

6. The teacher told us to write a procedure for the experiment.

7. The task took me a few minutes to complete.

8. Nadia tried it, but she had trouble.

9. Nadia asked us for help.

10. We gave her some suggestions.

B. **Write each sentence. Use the correct object pronoun in parentheses.**

11. That pollution experiment was easy for (I, me).

12. Mr. Thomas asked (I, me) about my experiment.

13. I told (him, he) about using polluted water to grow seeds.

14. I watered (them, they) daily with polluted water.

15. The plants did not enjoy (it, her).

16. I watered (they, them) until they wilted.

17. Students shared their results with (he, him).

18. Our teacher saw (they, them) and summarized the results.

19. Laurie showed (we, us) plants grown in artificial light.

20. It pleased (she, her) to see the results of the tests.

C. **Write each sentence. Replace the underlined word or words with the correct pronoun. Then write *SP* if the pronoun is a subject pronoun. Write *OP* if it is an object pronoun.**

21. Ms. Tobashi praised the class for a job well done.

22. Ms. Tobashi asked Ramona and me some questions.

23. My classmates and I discussed our discoveries.

24. Joe and Sasha were amazed at the results.

25. The class displayed the plants during Open House.

Colons and Hyphens

A. Write the word in each sentence that has a hyphen or a colon.

1. Our student council had a meeting at 3:00 P.M.

2. We met in the room near the west wing of the li-brary.

3. We had a half-hour meeting to discuss our funds.

4. The council included members from the fifth-grade class.

5. The president, Tabitha, is an eleven-year-old girl.

6. Her half-sister Kate drove us to the meeting.

7. The president called the meeting to order at 3:05.

8. About twenty-five students sat on the floor.

9. Our goal was to settle the mix-up over the money we'd made.

10. It was a nerve-racking meeting.

B. Write each sentence. Add hyphens or colons as needed.

11. I was a bleary eyed onlooker as the council debated.

12. The president was trying to maintain order as the audi ence murmured.

13. By 400 P.M., we still hadn't decided on a plan.

14. This face to face meeting wasn't getting us anywhere.

15. We discussed many important ideas, but we couldn't de cide on the best plan.

16. I suggested writing to the principal for a clear cut solution.

17. Our letter began "Dear Sir We hope you can advise us."

18. The principal would give us some top notch ideas.

19. We will give the money to a start up nursery.

20. It was 545 when we reached our decision.

C. Write each sentence. Use the correct word in parentheses. Underline words with hyphens or colons.

21. Are your problem-solving skills in (tiptop, tip-top) shape?

22. Do you make one-sided or (two sided, two-sided) decisions?

23. We need your decision by (530, 5:30) P.M., or by 6:00.

24. Ask your (brother-in-law, brother in law) or sister-in-law.

25. I like your self-control and your (first rate, first-rate) solution.

Extra Practice

Pronoun-Verb Agreement

A. Write *correct* if the underlined verb agrees with the subject pronoun. Write *incorrect* if it does not.

1. I enjoys the historical farm.
2. We visit this historical site every year.
3. It include a log cabin and a barnyard.
4. Inside the cabin, we see how people lived long ago.
5. She tells my brother historical facts about the tour.
6. He notice the handmade utensils in the kitchen.
7. We asks the tour guide about the tools.
8. She explains that pioneer families ate with wooden utensils.
9. She describes how pioneers made their own furniture.
10. Can you imagine having to make your own furniture?

B. Write each sentence. Use the correct form of the verb in parentheses.

11. We (look, looks) at each room of the old-fashioned cabin.
12. I (show, shows) my father the straw beds.
13. He (notice, notices) bedclothes made of woven fabrics.
14. We (watch, watches) a volunteer role-play a pioneer woman.
15. She (spin, spins) yarn from sheep's wool.
16. I (lead, leads) my brother to the workshop.
17. He (touch, touches) the hoe, the plow, and the other tools.
18. We both (see, sees) the corn mill.
19. I (ask, asks) the guide about this unusual tool.
20. She (demonstrate, demonstrates) how to grind corn.

C. Rewrite each sentence. Use the correct present-tense form of the word in parentheses.

21. I (describe) the tour to my friend.
22. She (help) me present a report to the class.
23. We (ask) the teacher about having a "Pioneer Day" celebration.
24. He (give) us permission to organize a festival.
25. It (become) the best event of the school year.

Combining Sentences: Subject and Object Pronouns

A. **Write the sentences. Underline the compound subject pronoun or compound object pronoun in each sentence.**

1. She and I decided to put on a play.

2. He and she wrote a script about famous explorers.

3. I asked him and her to hold auditions.

4. Mr. Lee helped them and me assign roles.

5. They and I appreciated the teacher's support.

6. She and he told the actors about the meeting.

7. You and I were filled with excitement.

8. He and I welcomed the actors to the meeting.

9. Sherry and the others asked him and me questions.

10. Devon helped her and them understand our plans.

B. **Write each sentence. Use the correct word in parentheses.**

11. He and (me, I) led the play rehearsals.

12. Actors asked (he, him) and me for help.

13. You and (I, me) know how challenging plays can be.

14. Ms. Reed saw (them, they) and me practice our parts.

15. I showed her and (them, they) the costumes.

16. Sherry reminded him and (me, I) about making sets.

17. (He, Him) and I persuaded Sherry to design the scenery.

18. (She, Her) and I gathered supplies and helpers.

19. Sherry showed them and (I, me) some sketches.

20. The sketches helped (she, her) and us design sets.

C. **Combine each pair of sentences by forming compound subjects or compound objects. Write each new sentence.**

21. He checked every detail. I checked every detail.

22. Sherry helped him. Sherry helped me.

23. She helped the others dress. I helped the others dress.

24. They were excited about the play. I was excited about the play.

25. The audience applauded for them. The audience applauded for me.

Extra Practice

Possessive Pronouns

A. Write the word in each sentence that is a possessive pronoun.

1. Our science teacher invited two meteorologists to class.

2. Mr. Otto introduced his guests.

3. The guests said their first names, Lorena and Vic.

4. Lorena spoke about her work at the station.

5. Vic explained his job of forecasting weather.

6. I know a coworker of theirs.

7. Vic and Lorena work with my dad.

8. Dad helps the meteorologists write their reports.

9. Our family watches the weather report together.

10. Does your family watch the broadcast, too?

B. Rewrite each sentence by using the correct possessive pronoun in parentheses.

11. Lorena and Vic shared (their, theirs) experiences.

12. Lorena liked (our, ours) questions.

13. I think (my, mine) was the best question of all.

14. I asked about the challenges of (they, their) work.

15. Vic said that (him, his) biggest challenge was waking up at 4:00 A.M.

16. Lorena said (her, hers) was keeping Vic awake.

17. (My, Mine) classmates asked questions about the weather.

18. Lorena and Vic talked about (their, theirs) favorite type of weather.

19. It was the same as (our, ours).

20. (Our, Ours) class thoroughly enjoyed the presentation.

C. Write each sentence. Replace the underlined word or words with the correct possessive pronoun.

21. Vic and Lorena's reports are based on satellite data.

22. Our class wants to visit Lorena's weather station.

23. Your class will visit the station next month.

24. We appreciated Vic's offer to tour the station.

25. The most interesting talk was Lorena's.

Contractions: Pronoun and Verb

A. **Write the two words that form each underlined contraction.**

1. It's the beginning of a new week.

2. I'm very happy about being in school today.

3. We're planning new projects with our teacher.

4. She's explaining the projects to her aides first.

5. They're listening to her very carefully.

6. Sometimes it's difficult for John to understand.

7. He's sitting in the back of the room.

8. We're asking our teacher if Mrs. Bailey will help us.

9. She's smiling at Mrs. Bailey and us now.

10. You're very pleased to have Mrs. Bailey's assistance.

B. **Write each sentence. Replace the underlined words with a contraction.**

11. We are starting a fifth-grade buddy system.

12. It is designed to help students in kindergarten.

13. Sometimes they are scared during the first few weeks of school.

14. I am sure the buddy system will be popular.

15. It is a great opportunity for fifth-grade students to help others.

16. She is going to have a "welcome party" to meet our buddies.

17. I know you are hoping to help Jorge.

18. He is a neighbor of mine.

19. I am interested in being buddies with Sumi.

20. I know we are alike.

C. **Write each sentence. Use the correct word.**

21. (Our, We're) helping Sumi and Jorge learn English.

22. (Their, They're) a bit shy and quiet.

23. (I'm, I) using puppets to teach them some words.

24. (Your, You're) using drawings to share your ideas.

25. (It's, Its) so rewarding being a buddy!

Extra Practice

Adjectives

A. **Write the noun that each underlined adjective describes.**

1. King James I sent about a <u>hundred</u> settlers to North America.

2. The king hoped to find gold and <u>other</u> riches.

3. The settlers left on a <u>cold</u> day in December of 1606.

4. Christopher Newport was the commander of the <u>three</u> ships.

5. The <u>small</u> vessels were named *Susan Constant*, *Godspeed*, and *Discovery*.

6. On May 14, 1607, the colonists sailed up the <u>marshy</u> James River.

7. The colonists settled in a <u>swampy</u> area they called Jamestown.

8. Jamestown was a <u>bad</u> location for a settlement.

9. Native tribes frequently attacked the <u>poor</u> colony.

10. <u>Many</u> settlers starved.

11. The <u>supply</u> boat arrived too late to save most of them.

12. In 1608, Captain John Smith became the <u>new</u> leader.

13. Smith was a <u>strong</u> captain who helped the settlers survive.

14. The winter of 1609 was <u>harsh</u> for the settlers.

15. Lord De La Warr became governor of the <u>new</u> settlement.

16. In 1614, a <u>wealthy</u> settler married Pocahontas.

17. Their marriage brought Jamestown eight <u>peaceful</u> years.

18. The <u>main</u> resources of the colony were tobacco, corn, and hogs.

19. Jamestown established the <u>first</u> legislature in North America.

20. It was the first permanent <u>British</u> settlement there.

Adjectives

B. **Write the sentences. Draw one line under each adjective. Draw two lines under the noun that the adjective describes.**

21. England was not the first country to colonize North America.

22. Brave colonists came from England, Scotland, Wales, and Ireland.

23. Some settlers came from France, Germany, and Spain.

24. Many colonists traveled to the Americas voluntarily.

25. However, slaves and orphans were forced to make the long journey.

26. Native Americans were already settled in the vast land.

27. The colonists traded various goods with them.

28. The adventurous British arrived later.

29. By the end of the colonial period, the British controlled North America.

C. **Write the sentences. Complete each sentence with an adjective.**

30. The colonists were _____ to settle in North America.

31. _____ people from different countries settled there.

32. People had _____ reasons to leave their homeland.

33. The colonists wanted _____ opportunities.

34. North America offered _____ land.

35. The colonists suffered _____ hardships to make their lives better.

36. _____ weather was one problem.

37. A _____ supply of food and water was another challenge.

38. Some colonists survived, but _____ colonists died.

39. The colonists learned _____ skills in order to survive.

40. Colonists worked together to build a _____ life.

Extra Practice

Articles

A. Write the sentences. Choose the correct article to complete each sentence.

1. How many types of clouds do you see in (a, the) sky?

2. What is (an, the) air temperature at the top of Mount Everest?

3. The Greenhouse Effect occurs when (a, the) atmosphere traps solar heat.

4. Ozone is (a, an) form of oxygen present in Earth's atmosphere.

5. Scientists believe that primitive Earth had (a, an) great deal of carbon dioxide in its atmosphere.

6. The stratosphere's upper boundary lies at (a, an) altitude of approximately 30 miles.

7. Earth has more oxygen than (a, the) other planets.

8. Volcanic dust in (the, a) atmosphere blocks sunlight.

9. What is (a, an) aerosol, and how does it affect the atmosphere?

10. (The, A) ionosphere reflects radio waves back to Earth.

B. Rewrite each sentence by using the correct article.

11. _____ thousand years ago, Iceland had a warmer climate.

12. Fossil fuels release carbon dioxide into _____ air.

13. Meteorologists can forecast the development of _____ hurricane.

14. A huge hurricane hit Galveston, _____ island off the Texas coast.

15. Do you know how cold fronts affect _____ weather?

16. Satellites are one of _____ tools meteorologists use to study weather.

17. _____ weather balloon can carry instruments 20 miles into the sky.

18. Stratus clouds are formed less than 6,000 feet from _____ earth.

19. _____ altostratus cloud has a smooth appearance.

20. During springtime, fog often forms early in _____ morning.

C. Write a sentence using each article. If the article is capitalized, use it as the first word in the sentence.

21. An   22. a   23. The   24. an   25. the

Demonstrative Adjectives

A. Write the demonstrative adjective in each underlined phrase.

1. <u>This year</u> we are studying geometry.

2. My teacher makes <u>that topic</u> easy to understand.

3. You can draw circles with <u>these instruments</u>.

4. Perpendicular lines are <u>those lines</u> that intersect at 90-degree angles.

5. I think <u>this shape</u> is a rhombus.

6. Can you tell if <u>that shape</u> is a polygon?

7. My partner thinks all <u>these rectangles</u> are similar.

8. If you add <u>those angles</u>, they measure 360 degrees.

9. <u>This triangle</u> is equilateral because all three sides are the same.

10. Draw a line with <u>those arrows</u> on the ends.

B. Write the demonstrative adjective in each sentence.

11. I need that ruler to measure the line.

12. These two trapezoids have the same measurements.

13. The teacher drew this angle as an example.

14. I used those sticks to form a parallelogram.

15. This point is called the vertex.

16. The triangle is a right triangle because those sides form a right angle.

17. We were asked to find these shapes in the classroom.

18. I liked that assignment because we were able to move around.

19. We had to find three examples of this shape.

20. This geometry chapter was really fun.

C. Rewrite each sentence by using *this*, *that*, *these*, or *those*.

21. "Please get _____ math tools on the table," Shawna said.

22. "How do I solve _____ problem?" Rod asked.

23. "You can use _____ tools," Shawna answered.

24. "_____ problem looks harder than this one," Rod said.

25. "Don't worry. We'll solve _____ problems together."

Extra Practice

Proper Adjectives

A. Write the proper adjective in each underlined phrase.

1. <u>Native American peoples</u> live in North America.

2. Jamestown was the first successful <u>British settlement</u>.

3. <u>Spanish conquistadors</u> explored Central America.

4. An <u>Asian emperor</u> sent an explorer to India.

5. <u>Portuguese sailors</u> traveled to South America.

6. <u>English shipbuilders</u> were the most skilled in their trade.

7. <u>French fur traders</u> traveled to western Canada.

8. Many <u>Swedish settlers</u> settled North America.

9. John Cabot, an <u>Italian navigator</u>, discovered Canada in 1497.

10. The Pacific was unknown to <u>European explorers</u>.

B. Write the sentences. Capitalize and underline each proper adjective.

11. The spanish Armada controlled the seas for many years.

12. Southern Mexico was settled by mayan peoples.

13. The Pacific Ocean was reached by dutch ships.

14. A chinese explorer made voyages to East Africa.

15. A french expedition discovered the St. Lawrence River in 1535.

16. chinese exploration stopped when the emperor had sailing ships destroyed.

17. Mounted police maintained order in canadian territories.

18. Lewis and Clark were american explorers.

19. John Ross was a scottish explorer.

20. Alaska was settled by russian explorers.

C. Complete each sentence with a proper adjective formed from the proper noun in parentheses.

21. Zheng He, a _____ explorer, made seven voyages. (China)

22. The _____ explorer Columbus sailed to the Americas. (Italy)

23. Ferdinand Magellan, a _____ explorer, led the first voyage around the world. (Portugal)

24. A _____ explorer looked for the Fountain of Youth. (Spain)

25. Powell led the first _____ group through the Grand Canyon. (America)

Comparative and Superlative Adjectives

A. Complete the list by writing the correct comparative or superlative adjective. Use your own sheet of paper.

1. round, rounder, _____

2. green, _____, greenest

3. smooth, _____, smoothest

4. fresh, fresher, _____

5. sad, _____, saddest

6. sweet, _____, sweetest

7. strong, stronger, _____

8. busy, _____, busiest

9. bright, _____, brightest

10. heavy, heavier, _____

B. Write each sentence. Choose the correct adjective from the pair in parentheses.

11. The Mississippi River is the (longer, longest) river in the United States.

12. Lake Michigan is (larger, largest) than Lake Erie.

13. The Pacific Ocean is (bigger, biggest) than the Atlantic Ocean.

14. Rhode Island is the (smaller, smallest) state.

15. The (colder, coldest) temperatures are often in Alaska.

16. The Grand Canyon is (deeper, deepest) than any other canyon in the world.

17. Mount Mitchell is the (higher, highest) point east of the Mississippi.

18. Yellowstone National Park has some of the (prettier, prettiest) scenery in the country.

19. The Appalachians are the (older, oldest) mountains in North America.

20. Death Valley is the (drier, driest) place in the United States.

C. Write each sentence. Use the correct form of the adjective in parentheses.

21. This geography game is (easy) than the last one we played.

22. These are the (hard) question cards!

23. What is the (wide) river in the world?

24. Your question was (tough) than mine.

25. I am the (great) game player in the world!

Extra Practice

Comparing with *More* and *Most*

A. Complete the list by writing the missing form of each adjective. Use your own sheet of paper.

1. interesting, more interesting, _____

2. expressive, more expressive, _____

3. creative, _____, most creative

4. difficult, _____, most difficult

5. stable, more stable, _____

6. dangerous, _____, most dangerous

7. capable, _____, most capable

8. believable, more believable, _____

9. reliable, more reliable, _____

10. creative, _____, most creative

B. Read each adjective. Write the form of the adjective you would use to compare two nouns. Then write the form you would use to compare more than two nouns.

11. crowded

12. educated

13. courageous

14. personal

15. useful

16. imaginative

17. beautiful

18. terrifying

19. amusing

20. spectacular

C. Write each sentence. Use the correct form of the adjective in parentheses.

21. A Michigan winter is (frigid) than a Florida winter.

22. The Great Banks provide some of the world's (plentiful) fishing.

23. Ontario's Point Pelee is one of the (beautiful) parts of southern Canada.

24. The Lowlands area is (suitable) for growing grain than for mining.

25. One of the (rugged) regions in the United States is the Rockies.

Comparing with *Good* and *Bad*

A. **Write each sentence. Choose the correct word in parentheses.**

1. A computer is one of the (better, best) tools for looking up information.

2. Searching Web sites may be (better, best) than skimming through books.

3. The (worse, worst) computers take several minutes to find information.

4. The (better, best) computers find information fast.

5. Nothing is (worse, worst) than seeing incorrect information on a Web site.

6. It is (better, best) to use several resources than just one.

7. The (better, best) approach is to use both online and print resources.

8. The (worse, worst) plan is to use only one source of information.

9. The more resources you use, the (better, best).

10. My work is (better, best) when I use a variety of sources.

B. **Write the sentences. Complete each sentence with the correct form of *good* or *bad*.**

11. The (good) decision I ever made was to use a computer for my research.

12. I wrote a (good) research report this year than last year.

13. I used to be much (bad) at using the computer.

14. With practice, I got much (good) at it.

15. I use my new skills to find the (good) facts for my report.

16. Some sources are (bad) than others.

17. I had the (bad) time finding Web sites until I used search engines.

18. Search engines made my life a lot (good)!

19. Search engines work the (good) when you input keywords.

20. I used to think research was the (bad) task, but now I love it!

C. **Use each of these forms of *good* or *bad* in a sentence. Write the new sentence.**

21. good   **22.** better   **23.** best   **24.** worse   **25.** worst

Extra Practice

Adverbs

A. **Write whether the underlined adverb tells *how*, *when*, or *where*.**

1. The sun was shining <u>brightly</u>.
2. The parrots were squawking <u>loudly</u>.
3. One red bird was <u>nearby</u>.
4. <u>Lately</u>, birds have fascinated me.
5. I <u>happily</u> watched a blue macaw.
6. My sister <u>always</u> wants to see the peacocks.
7. <u>Afterward</u>, we strolled to the reptile house.
8. Mother stared <u>cautiously</u> at the python.
9. We <u>quietly</u> observed the tree snake.
10. We went <u>outside</u>.

B. **Write each sentence. Draw one line under the adverb and two lines under the verb it describes.**

11. We drove slowly through the jungle area.
12. Monkeys swung playfully from the trees.
13. Parrots screeched loudly at the people.
14. One bright bird flew overhead.
15. Its feathers shone radiantly.
16. I always enjoy the animal park.
17. We saw a pride of lions next.
18. Immediately, a lion roared.
19. Lions can hunt skillfully.
20. The pride rested lazily in the sun.

C. **Write each sentence. Draw one line under the adverb. Write whether the underlined adverb tells *how*, *when*, or *where*.**

21. A pack of gazelles leaped gracefully.
22. We walked ahead to see more animals.
23. Soon we had seen the whole park.
24. Finally, Dad said that it was time to go.
25. I sadly waved good-bye to the animals.

Adverbs Before Adjectives and Adverbs

A. **Write the adverb that describes the underlined word.**

1. Families had extremely <u>tight</u> quarters on the ship.

2. The crew moved extraordinarily <u>fast</u>.

3. The children felt utterly <u>frightened</u>.

4. The weather became stormy quite <u>quickly</u>.

5. The winds were outrageously <u>fierce</u>.

6. The wind howled very <u>loudly</u>.

7. Lightning struck the ship almost <u>immediately</u>.

8. Very <u>dark</u> clouds filled the sky.

9. The rain stopped rather <u>suddenly</u>.

10. The storm was completely <u>over</u>.

B. **Add an adverb to describe each of the following words. Use an adverb only once.**

11. difficult

12. excited

13. tired

14. visible

15. carefully

16. nervous

17. ready

18. slowly

19. dusty

20. damp

C. **Write each sentence. Write whether the underlined adverb describes an adjective or another adverb.**

21. The ship bumped <u>too</u> heavily against the dock.

22. The passengers were <u>incredibly</u> quiet.

23. The people gathered their things <u>quite</u> slowly.

24. The departure line was <u>extremely</u> long.

25. The crowd was <u>rather</u> noisy.

Comparing with Adverbs

A. **Write the correct adverb form to compare two actions. Then write the adverb form that compares three or more actions.**

1. slowly
2. early
3. quickly
4. swiftly
5. often
6. loudly
7. fast
8. late
9. softly
10. poorly

B. **Write the sentences. Underline the adverb that compares in each sentence.**

11. The eagle can see more clearly than a human can see.
12. Some animals can run longer than other animals.
13. The cheetah runs the fastest of all over short distances.
14. A mare eats grain more often than a pony does.
15. One calf walked more slowly than the other calf.
16. The tree frog hid most carefully of all.
17. The raccoon climbed higher than the bear.
18. The gazelle moved more quickly than the lion.
19. I think the lion is the most skillful hunter of all.
20. The crab moves more cautiously than the scorpion.

C. **Write each sentence. Choose the correct comparative or superlative adverb from the parentheses.**

21. The ladybug moved (more slowly, most slowly) than the ant.
22. The beetle moved the (fastest, faster) of all the insects.
23. The housefly flew (most quickly, more quickly) than the moth.
24. The trap-door spider hunts (most skillfully, more skillfully) than the common house spider.
25. The spider spins its web (more skillfully, most skillfully) of all.

Negatives

A. **Write the negative in each sentence.**

1. No one in the group had flown before.

2. Nobody wanted to board the plane.

3. Briana doesn't have the tickets.

4. Never had we been so confused.

5. Scott didn't have the tickets, either.

6. I don't know where the tickets are.

7. They weren't in anyone's pocket.

8. No solution could be found.

9. "Aren't those the tickets?" asked Sandy.

10. Nothing more needed to be said.

B. **Choose a word from the Word Bank to rewrite each sentence.**

no	wasn't	never	weren't	hadn't
couldn't	None	No one	nowhere	Nothing

11. We _____ wait for our ride in the glider.

12. A glider has _____ motor.

13. The plane_____ as noisy as I had expected.

14. _____ else is quite like a ride in a glider.

15. _____ wanted to get off the plane.

16. I had _____ done anything more exciting.

17. Our town was _____ in sight.

18. The clouds _____ far above us.

19. We _____ been flying long when it was time to land.

20. _____ of us regretted the trip.

C. **Write each sentence. Change one of the negatives in each sentence to a positive word so that the sentence is correct.**

21. Nobody doesn't want the trip to end.

22. We didn't have no more money.

23. They didn't know nothing else to do.

24. I don't want to do nothing more.

25. I haven't no more ideas.

Extra Practice

Punctuation in Dialogue

A. Write the sentences. Underline the name of the person who is speaking in each sentence. Circle the quotation marks.

1. "Let's make paper helicopters," announced Kelsey.

2. Riley asked, "What do we need?"

3. "First, we need paper," answered Jenna.

4. "We also need scissors," added Mario.

5. "Did Mario say we also need scissors?" asked Graciela.

6. "Yes," answered Jenna. "Now let's each make a helicopter."

7. "What do we do first?" asked Riley.

8. "Fold your paper in half," said Mario.

9. "Don't just say to fold it in half!" exclaimed Jenna.

10. "Then unfold it," confirmed Mario, "and cut along the fold on each side."

11. "Do I cut it only a third of the way?" asked Riley.

12. Mario said, "Yes, and then fold in each side."

13. "Wow!" said Riley. "Now it looks like a giant letter *T*."

14. "Cut the top down to the fold line and in half," said Graciela.

15. "It looks like rabbit ears now," laughed Mario.

16. Jenna continued, "Fold one flap back and one forward."

17. "Put a paper clip on the bottom," instructed Kelsey.

18. "Hold it up high," said Mario, "and release it."

19. "Oh," Graciela noticed, "it spins like a helicopter now!"

20. "What fun this is!" Jenna shouted.

B. **Write each sentence. Draw one line under the direct quotation.**

21. Mom said, "We're going to the Smithsonian Institution."

22. "Will we go during vacation?" I asked.

23. "Yes," she answered, "we leave next Tuesday."

24. "What will we see?" inquired my sister.

25. My brother answered, "Nothing fun will be there, I bet."

26. "We will go to the National Air and Space Museum," said Dad.

27. "What do they have there?" asked my brother.

28. "They have a model of the Wright brothers' plane," Mom replied.

29. "They have one of the space capsules," I added.

30. "Do they have a capsule from a lunar landing?" my brother asked in surprise.

C. **Write each sentence. Use capitalization and punctuation correctly.**

31. the museum really has a space capsule said Dad.

32. I said they also have the *Spirit of St. Louis.*

33. is that Charles Lindbergh's plane? asked my brother.

34. yes I replied and they also have many uniforms.

35. my brother cried what fun this is going to be!

36. now do you want to go? I asked.

37. My brother responded when do we leave?

38. go pack your bag said Mom.

39. did Mom say go pack your bag?

40. I think we're going to enjoy this trip commented Dad.

Extra Practice

Prepositions

A. Write the sentences. Underline each preposition.

1. My friend and I stopped at the park.

2. We ate lunch on the grass.

3. I had ice in my juice.

4. My friend poured water into a bottle.

5. We sat beside a maple tree.

6. The sun peeked through a cloud.

7. The birds flew among the branches.

8. Cyclists rode by us.

9. People were jogging around the track.

10. Children stood between their parents.

B. Write the sentences. Choose a preposition to complete each sentence.

11. Two girls played catch _____ us.

12. A ball rolled _____ the fence.

13. The team _____ the infield wore red.

14. The team at bat had blue hats _____ their heads.

15. One player hit the ball _____ the park.

16. The player jumped _____ the fence.

17. He returned _____ the home run was scored.

18. We sat _____ home plate.

19. We stayed _____ noon.

20. Then we ate hamburgers _____ lunch.

C. Use each preposition in a sentence. Write the new sentences.

21. across

22. beside

23. over

24. between

25. among

Prepositional Phrases

A. **Write the prepositional phrase in each sentence. The preposition is underlined to help you.**

1. The heart is located <u>inside</u> the rib cage.

2. The ribs protect the heart <u>from</u> damage.

3. The heart is a muscle <u>in</u> the circulatory system.

4. The heart is positioned <u>under</u> the breastbone.

5. You feel your heart beat <u>against</u> your chest.

6. <u>After</u> a race, your heart beats rapidly.

7. Your heart beats more slowly <u>during</u> sleep.

8. Blood carries oxygen <u>to</u> your cells.

9. Blood carries wastes <u>from</u> the cells.

10. The heart is an important part <u>of</u> the body.

B. **Write each sentence. Draw one line under the prepositional phrase.**

11. Our teacher showed us a video about exercise.

12. During exercise, you should check your pulse.

13. Put your finger on your pulse.

14. You can count how many times your heart beats in one minute.

15. After exercise, your heart beats faster.

16. Blood is pumping more quickly through your veins.

17. Exercise is good for your body.

18. I like to run around the school track.

19. My best friend likes to play basketball inside the school gym.

20. My mom likes to jog near our house.

C. **Write each sentence. Draw one line under the prepositional phrase. Draw two lines under the preposition.**

21. Exercise takes care of your heart.

22. With exercise, your body is healthier.

23. You can choose from many different exercises.

24. Less oxygen is needed during rest.

25. Exercise is necessary for good health.

Extra Practice

Combining Sentences: Complex Sentences

A. Write the conjunction that joins the two ideas in each complex sentence.

1. We made a plan when we planted our vegetables.
2. We planted carrots because we like them.
3. I brought radish seeds since they grow easily.
4. Pearleen planted peas before she watered the ground.
5. Peas grow well unless the weather is hot.
6. We raked rocks although some pebbles remained.
7. We patted the soil after we placed the seeds.
8. We worked hard until it was noon.
9. We would take a break if we could.
10. I stopped working as the sun went down.

B. Write each sentence. Circle the conjunction. Draw one line under each of the two ideas in the sentence.

11. Pearleen adds compost because it helps the plants to grow.
12. I watered the ground after the seeds were soaked.
13. I can't wait until the vegetables are ready.
14. We can pick them as they mature.
15. Tomatoes are ripe when they are red.
16. The peas will be ready after the pods are full.
17. Pearleen added a trellis where she knew the plants would climb.
18. Radishes are ready more quickly than you think.
19. The carrots won't be ready if we watch them grow.
20. We will pull out the plants after the first frost comes.

C. Combine each pair of sentences into one complex sentence. Use the conjunction in parentheses. Write the new sentence.

21. I won't plant beets. I don't like them. (because)
22. Plants grow fast. The weather is hot. (when)
23. The garden needed water. The heat wave was over. (after)
24. I added fertilizer. I raked the soil. (before)
25. I like to garden. I really am not a gardener. (although)

Commas with Prepositional Phrases and Interjections

A. Write each sentence. Underline the prepositional phrase or the interjection. Circle the commas.

1. During the afternoon, the sun is hot.

2. Before the game, I get my sunscreen.

3. Wow, the sun is hot!

4. At midday, I rested.

5. To our picnic, we brought an umbrella.

6. Gee, too much sun might give me wrinkles.

7. Inside the park, I touched poison oak.

8. On my hand, I began to itch.

9. In a few minutes, the poison oak spread.

10. For my rash, my mother applied lotion.

B. Write each sentence. Underline the prepositional phrase or the interjection.

11. Oh! Goose bumps look funny.

12. During cold weather, I get goose bumps.

13. Gee, I better wear a sweater.

14. Well, I don't have goose bumps anymore.

15. Oh my, what happens if I cut my skin?

16. In a cut, a clot seals the wound.

17. With white blood cells, the infection is attacked.

18. At the edges, skin cells begin to grow.

19. Over time, new skin cells close the wound.

20. Wow, skin is amazing!

C. Write each sentence. Add a comma to prevent misreading.

21. After stretching skin holds its shape.

22. On skin wrinkles are found.

23. Look oil keeps our skin waterproof.

24. To our skin pigment gives color.

25. With sunscreen protection starts.

Build Skills

Note-Taking and Summarizing

DEFINITIONS AND FEATURES

- You can take notes from written material or from listening to a speaker.
- When taking notes, record only important facts. Use your own words instead of the author's or speaker's words.
- Record the sources of your notes, including the book title, the author, and the page number.
- You can summarize your notes to be sure that you understand the material. A summary includes only the most important ideas.

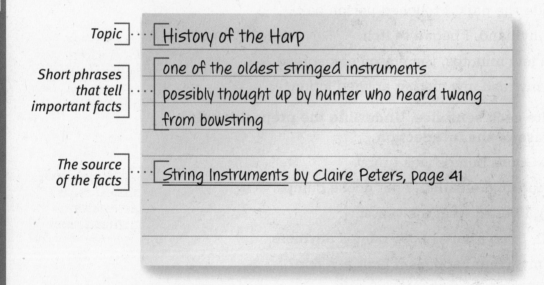

Topic ···· History of the Harp

Short phrases that tell important facts ···· one of the oldest stringed instruments
possibly thought up by hunter who heard twang from bowstring

The source of the facts ···· String Instruments by Claire Peters, page 41

Practice Take notes on the following article, listing five facts on a sheet of paper. Then write a summary using your notes and your own words. Give your summary a title.

The modern concert harp is the only instrument in an orchestra that is played entirely by plucking the strings. Harpists use their fingers to pluck the 47 strings. Modern concert harps have seven foot-pedals. Each pedal has three possible positions. These pedals change the pitch of the strings. This allows the harpist to play in any key.

Choosing Reference Sources for Research

DEFINITIONS AND FEATURES

- Use two or more sources when researching information for a research report.
- Sources could include nonfiction books, periodicals (magazines and newspapers), encyclopedias, interviews, and videotapes.
- Choose the source that matches your topic. For current information, use a magazine. For statistics, use an almanac.
- Include a bibliography, or list of sources, at the end of the report. Include title, author, and date of publication of each source.

Use two or more sources when researching.

List the title and author, as well as the date of publication and page numbers, in a bibliography.

Practice Read the following topics. Write *book, periodical, encyclopedia, video, audio recording,* or *interview* to name the best source of information for that topic.

1. A local architect's plan for a new park in your town

2. A brief article on elm trees

3. Large amounts of specific, in-depth information about baseball

4. The local weather report for the week

5. The most current information about campgrounds

6. Instructions for building a birdhouse

7. A diagram of the anatomy of a fish

8. A recording of a poet reciting nature poems

9. The life of a famous author

10. How to make a specific recipe created by your mother

Build Skills

Parts of a Book

DEFINITIONS AND FEATURES

- The table of contents lists chapter titles and page numbers. It can give you an idea of the chapters' main ideas.
- The copyright page tells the company who published the book and the date and place of publication.
- The glossary is a dictionary that lists words found in a particular book.
- Use the index to find specific information in the book. The index lists topics and subtopics in alphabetical order.

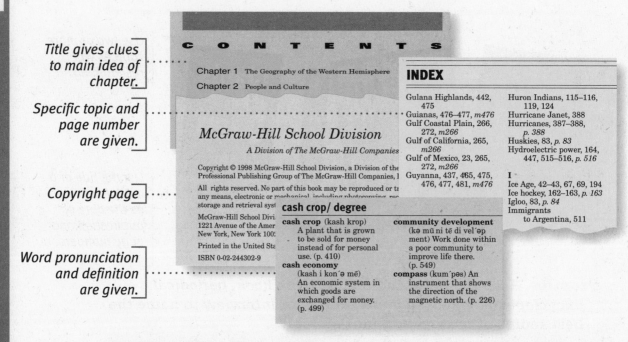

Title gives clues to main idea of chapter.

Specific topic and page number are given.

Copyright page

Word pronunciation and definition are given.

Practice Write *table of contents, copyright page, glossary,* or *index* to tell where in a book you would locate the following information.

1. The meaning of the word *thorax*

2. Page numbers for information about the red ant

3. A date to tell whether a book is more than five years old

4. Page numbers for information about air pressure

5. Where a book was published

Encyclopedia

DEFINITIONS AND FEATURES

- An **encyclopedia** is a print or electronic reference source that includes information about people, places, things, and events.
- **Articles** in encyclopedias are about specific topics.
- Within each encyclopedia, articles are arranged in **alphabetical order** by **keywords**. Each keyword is the main topic of the article.
- Encyclopedia **volumes** are arranged in alphabetical order.
- **Guide words** at the top of the page tell you the first article and last article on the page.

Use this volume to find articles about people, places, things, and events that begin with S.

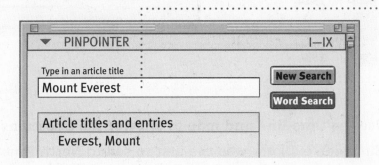

After entering keyword(s), press the ENTER key and a list of articles will appear.

Practice Write the keyword or words that you would look up or type to find information about each subject.

1. Musical instruments in the string section of an orchestra

2. Organs of the respiratory system

3. The art of Winslow Homer

4. The rain forests of Brazil

5. Birthplace of author E. B. White

Build Skills

Time Lines and Historical Maps

DEFINITIONS AND FEATURES

- A time line shows the order in which events happened. Dates are written on a time line to show the period of time between events.
- A historical map shows land features and places from long ago. It may show where historical events occurred. Historical maps often include labels or symbols that convey important information.

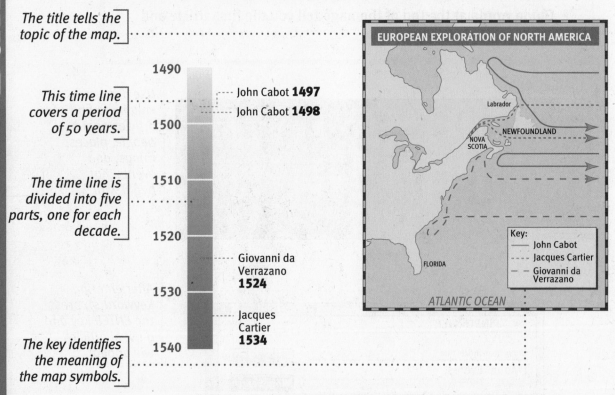

The title tells the topic of the map.

This time line covers a period of 50 years.

The time line is divided into five parts, one for each decade.

The key identifies the meaning of the map symbols.

1490
1500
1510
1520
1530
1540

John Cabot **1497**
John Cabot **1498**

Giovanni da Verrazano **1524**

Jacques Cartier **1534**

EUROPEAN EXPLORATION OF NORTH AMERICA

Labrador

NEWFOUNDLAND

NOVA SCOTIA

FLORIDA

ATLANTIC OCEAN

Key:
John Cabot
Jacques Cartier
Giovanni da Verrazano

Practice Use the time line and map to answer the questions.

1. What European explorer was the first to sail to North America during this time period?

2. Did you use the time line or the map to answer question 1? Why?

3. What explorer followed the most southerly route?

4. Why can't you use the time line to answer question 3?

5. Which explorer sailed to North America twice? How do you know?

Graphs

Build Skills

DEFINITIONS AND FEATURES

- A **graph** is a visual way to show information. Graphs help readers **compare** different types of information, or data.
- The **title** tells what information can be found on the graph.
- **Labels** on graphs give more information about the data.
- There are many **types of graphs**. **Circle graphs** show how a group can be divided into smaller groups. **Bar graphs** show numbers. Each bar represents a number of items.

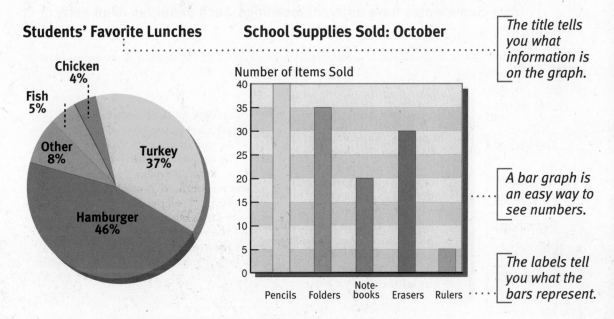

Students' Favorite Lunches

Chicken 4%
Fish 5%
Other 8%
Turkey 37%
Hamburger 46%

School Supplies Sold: October

Number of Items Sold

Pencils Folders Note-books Erasers Rulers

The title tells you what information is on the graph.

A bar graph is an easy way to see numbers.

The labels tell you what the bars represent.

Practice Use both graphs to answer the questions.

1. Which lunch do students like the most?

2. Which lunch do students like the least?

3. Which lunches do students like about the same?

4. Do more students like hamburger, or do more students like chicken, fish, and "other" lunches combined?

5. What clue helps you answer question 4 without adding?

6. How many notebooks were sold during October?

7. Which item had the highest sales?

8. Which item had 30 sales?

9. How many more notebooks were sold than rulers?

10. How are the two graphs different from each other?

Build Skills

Dictionary

DEFINITIONS AND FEATURES

- A dictionary can help you learn the meaning, spelling, and pronunciation of an unfamiliar word.
- The words in dark type are called entry words. They show the spelling and syllables of the words.
- The two guide words at the top of a dictionary page identify the first entry word and the last entry word on that page.
- Entry words are arranged in alphabetical order.
- The pronunciation is shown in parentheses.
- Some words have different meanings. Each definition of an entry word is numbered.

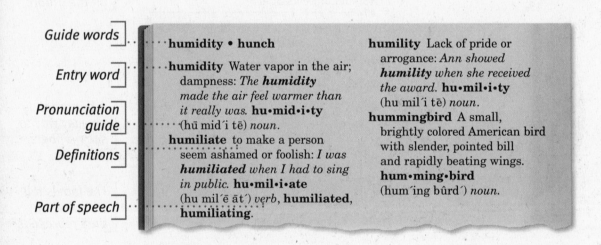

Guide words
Entry word
Pronunciation guide
Definitions
Part of speech

humidity • hunch

humidity Water vapor in the air; dampness: *The humidity made the air feel warmer than it really was.* **hu•mid•i•ty** (hū mid´i tē) *noun.*
humiliate to make a person seem ashamed or foolish: *I was humiliated when I had to sing in public.* **hu•mil•i•ate** (hu mil´ē āt´) *verb,* **humiliated,** **humiliating.**

humility Lack of pride or arrogance: *Ann showed humility when she received the award.* **hu•mil•i•ty** (hu mil´i tē) *noun.*
hummingbird A small, brightly colored American bird with slender, pointed bill and rapidly beating wings. **hum•ming•bird** (hum´ing bûrd´) *noun.*

Practice Use the above entries from part of a dictionary to answer these questions.

1. What part of speech is the word *humidity*?

2. How many syllables does the word *humiliate* have?

3. What word could you look up to further understand the meaning of *humility*?

4. Which of these words would appear elsewhere on this dictionary page: *hunch, human, humus, hunger, hurdle*?

5. Why are the words *humiliated* and *humiliating* shown after the entry word *humiliate*?

Build Skills

Thesaurus

DEFINITIONS AND FEATURES

- A **thesaurus** is a reference source that lists synonyms and antonyms. **Synonyms** are words that have the same or similar meanings. **Antonyms** are words that have opposite meanings.
- Use a thesaurus to help you choose more interesting and more exact words to use in your writing.
- Synonyms are listed after **entry words** in a thesaurus. Entry words in dark type are listed in alphabetical order.
- Some entries include a **cross-reference**, which refers you to other words in the thesaurus.
- A **computer or an online thesaurus** can usually be found under "Tools" in the menu bar of a word-processing program.

Practice Write each sentence. Replace the underlined word with a synonym or an antonym shown in the thesaurus entries on this page. Use a different word each time.

1. Amy was <u>making</u> a collage.

2. She heard a <u>loud</u> voice.

3. She <u>looked</u> out the window.

4. A man was <u>making</u> a speech.

5. The crowd around him was <u>loud</u>.

Build Skills

Card Catalog

DEFINITIONS AND FEATURES

- A card catalog provides information about each library book. It may be a set of cards or a computer database.
- The cards in the catalog are listed in alphabetical order.
- Each book has three cards stored in separate files: an author card, a title card, and a subject card.
- The author card lists the name of the author first. The title card lists the title of the book first. The subject card lists the general subject of the book first.
- The call number tells where to find the book on the shelf.

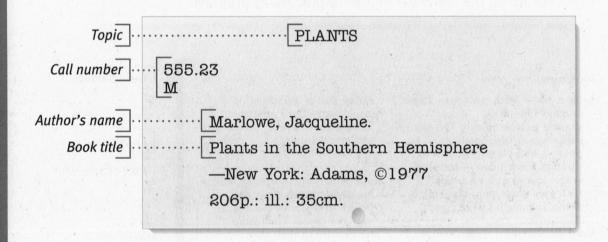

Topic .... PLANTS

Call number 555.23
M

Author's name ..... Marlowe, Jacqueline.

Book title ..... Plants in the Southern Hemisphere
—New York: Adams, ©1977
206p.: ill.: 35cm.

Practice Look at the subject card on this page to answer the following questions. Write your answers on a sheet of paper.

1. Who is the author of the book?
2. What is the title of the book?
3. What is the call number of the book?
4. What is the subject of the book?
5. What year was the book published?

Library or Media Center

DEFINITIONS AND FEATURES

- A library or a media center includes a variety of materials and resources that are arranged in different sections.
- Fiction books are arranged on shelves alphabetically by authors' last names. Nonfiction books are arranged by subject.
- The circulation desk is where you check out books.
- The reference section includes books for research such as encyclopedias, atlases, and almanacs. The reference section may also include computers for Internet and CD-ROM research.
- A media center may include video and audio recordings, playback machines, and software.
- The card catalog contains information about library books. It may be in drawers or on a computer database.
- The periodicals section includes magazines and newspapers.

Library Floor Plan

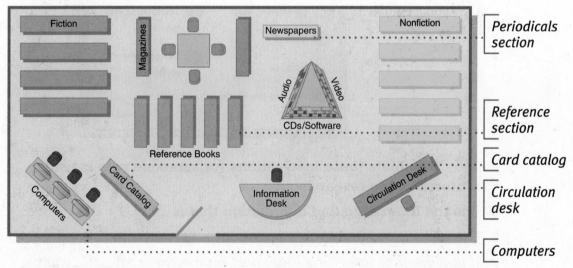

Practice **Look at the floor plan shown on this page. Write where you would find each of the following items in the library.**

1. the *A* volume of an encyclopedia

2. a list of Roald Dahl books that can be found in the library

3. a Web site on how to play chess

4. an issue of *Sports Illustrated for Kids*

5. a copy of *The Giver* by Lois Lowry

Build Skills

Build Skills

Using the Internet

DEFINITIONS AND FEATURES

- The Internet is an up-to-the-minute, current source of information about many topics.
- You can use a search engine to find information about a specific topic. Narrow your search by using keywords.
- Online encyclopedias contain the same type of information as print encyclopedias. They are often arranged alphabetically by keyword.
- You can find daily news on the Internet by searching through online newspapers.
- At some Web sites, you can send e-mail to experts to ask specific questions about topics.

You can use a search engine to find information about a topic.

Kids' Info

Topic

DOWNLOAD
SEARCH

- Homework Help
- Sports
- Science
- All Over the World
- Technology and Games
- Entertainment News

HELP!

Practice Complete these instructions for someone who is using the Internet to do research.

1. Use the Internet to find information that is _____.

2. Use a _____ to find Web sites about a certain topic.

3. If you want to interview an expert online, you can _____ him or her.

4. Use _____ to find Web sites and encyclopedia articles on specific topics.

5. If you want to find out what has happened in a certain city on a certain day, check out an online _____.

Periodicals and Media Resources

DEFINITIONS AND FEATURES

- **Periodicals** are magazines and newspapers published at regular intervals, such as weekly, monthly, and quarterly.
- Periodicals provide current information about various topics.
- The Readers' Guide to Periodical Literature is a set of books or an electronic database that alphabetically lists, by topic or author, articles published in magazines. It identifies the magazine, issue, and pages where the article can be found.
- Media resources are nonprint resources that you can use to find information, such as CD-ROMs, video, and audio recordings.

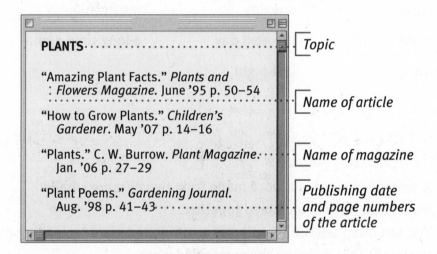

PLANTS · — *Topic*

"Amazing Plant Facts." *Plants and
  Flowers Magazine.* June '95 p. 50–54 · · · · — *Name of article*

"How to Grow Plants." *Children's
  Gardener.* May '07 p. 14–16

"Plants." C. W. Burrow. *Plant Magazine.* · · — *Name of magazine*
  Jan. '06 p. 27–29

"Plant Poems." *Gardening Journal.* · · · · · · · · · — *Publishing date
  Aug. '98 p. 41–43 · · · · · · · · · · · · · · · · · · and page numbers
  of the article*

Practice Use the *Readers' Guide* entries on this screen to answer the following questions.

1. How many magazines include articles about plants?

2. What magazine has an article titled "Plants"?

3. What article is in the magazine *Children's Gardener*?

4. When was the article "Amazing Plant Facts" published?

5. On what pages will you find the article titled "Plant Poems"?

Build Skills

RULE 1 — **Time-Order Words**

- A time-order word tells when events happen and in what order they happen.

- Use time-order words to show how ideas are related to each other and to make your writing flow more smoothly.

- Sometimes a phrase can show time order in a piece of writing.

first	yesterday	now
next	today	before
then	tomorrow	after
last	as soon as	in the meantime
finally	one day	meanwhile
second	the next day	a long time ago
third	last night	

RULE 2 — **Compound Words**

- A compound word is a word made from two or more smaller words that have been joined together.
- You can often tell the meaning of a compound word by looking at the words that make up the compound word.
- A compound word may be written as one word, two or more words separated by a hyphen, or as two separate words.

Two Words	Compound Word	Meaning
fire + truck	fire truck	truck that fights fires
back + pack	backpack	pack worn on the back
space + shuttle	space shuttle	shuttle that flies into space
fish + hook	fishhook	hook that catches fish
pot + roast	pot roast	roast made in a pot
wall + paper	wallpaper	paper placed on the wall
double + park	double-park	park two cars next to each other

RULE 3

Prefixes and Suffixes

- **Prefixes** and **suffixes** are word parts added to the beginning or end of a **root word** or **base word**.
- A **prefix** is a word part added to the beginning of a base word.
- A **suffix** is a word part added to the end of a base word.
- Adding a prefix or suffix changes the **meaning** of the base word to which it is added.

Prefix	Meaning	Suffix	Meaning
re-	again, back	-ful	full of
un-, dis-, non-	not, the opposite of	-able, -ible	capable or worthy of, fit for
mis-	wrongly, badly	-ness	state, condition, or quality of
pre-	before	-less	without, not having
bi-	having two of; twice	-ist	one who does or makes
im-, in-	not, without, in, into	-ment	the act, state, quality, or result of

RULE 4

Synonyms and Antonyms

- **Synonyms** are words that have the **same** or almost the same meanings.
- **Antonyms** are words that have **opposite** meanings.
- A word may have **more than one** synonym or antonym.

Word	Synonym	Antonym
strong	powerful	weak
careful	cautious	careless
fix	repair	destroy
untrue	false	true
possible	likely	impossible

Build Skills

RULE 5

Word Choice

- Writers carefully **choose words** to create vivid pictures for their readers and to use words with the **exact meanings** they intend.
- Choose a **synonym** that best expresses your meaning.
- Select **vivid verbs** and **vivid adjectives** to create stronger and more exact descriptions.

Vague Verbs	Precise Verbs	Vague Adjectives	Precise Adjectives
ask	invite	big	mammoth
do	perform	cold	frigid
fix	remodel	dark	foggy
fly	soar	dull	uninteresting
get	reach	fast	speedy
hang	drape	fine	splendid
look	peer	hard	puzzling
melt	liquefy	late	overdue
move	dance	nice	agreeable
say	shout	noisy	ear-splitting
		old	outmoded
		sweet	honeyed

Build Skills

RULE 6

Figurative Language

- **Figurative language** uses words in ways beyond their usual or literal meanings.
- Writers use figurative language to **create images** for readers.
- Figurative language can make writing more **vivid**, **precise**, and **interesting**.
- **Similes**, **metaphors**, and **personification** are three specific types of figurative language.

Figurative Language	Definition	Example
simile	compares using the word *like* or *as*	The beach was *as hot as an oven*. The students' footsteps sounded *like thunder*.
metaphor	compares two unlike things without using words of comparison	The beach *was an oven*. The students' footsteps *were thunder* on the stairs.
personification	gives human qualities to animals, ideas, and objects	The cool water *invited* me to jump in. The stairs *complained* when the students ran up them.

Build Skills

Problem Words

● The English language includes some confusing words that are often misused. The following charts will help you understand how to use these words properly.

Words	Correct Usage
accept	*Accept* means "to receive" or "to agree to." It is a verb. *I accept your apology.*
except	*Except* means "other than." It is usually a preposition. *I like all fruits* except *bananas.*
bad	*Bad* is an adjective. It means "the opposite of good." *My brother is a* bad *cook because he never reads directions.*
badly	*Badly* is an adverb. It means "in a bad manner." *The boy treated his sister* badly *because his feelings were hurt.*
beside	*Beside* means "on the side of." *The book is* beside *the lamp.*
besides	*Besides* means "in addition to." Besides *Joel, Carl and Ellen were cast in the play.*
can	*Can* tells about an ability. *I* can *play the flute.*
may	*May* expresses permission. *You* may *spend the night at Harold's house.*
fewer	*Fewer* is used for things that can be counted. *I have* fewer *crayons than Todd does.*
less	*Less* is used for things or ideas that cannot be counted. *I am* less *organized than Sherry is.*
good	*Good* is an adjective that describes something positive. *I had a* good *steak at the restaurant last night.*
well	Well is usually an adverb. It gives more information about the verb by telling "how." *My sister swam* well *last summer.*

Problem Words

Words	Correct Usage
lay	*Lay* means "to put something down." Lay *the papers on my desk.*
lie	*Lie* means "to recline or rest." *Seth* lies *on the floor in front of the fireplace.*
loose	*Loose* means "not secured." *Maggie had her first* loose *tooth.*
lose	*Lose* means "to misplace." It is a verb. *Did you* lose *your house key?*
set	*Set* means "to put something down or in a certain place." *I* set *my pencil on the table.*
sit	*Sit* means "to be seated." *Our class should* sit *in the front of the auditorium.*
their	*Their* is a possessive pronoun meaning "belonging to them." *The Murphys are gone, so Ryan will feed* their *dog.*
they're	*They're* is a contraction meaning "they are." *We aren't sure when* they're *coming back from vacation.*
your	*Your* is a possessive pronoun that means "something that belongs to you." *Is that* your *cat?*
you're	*You're* is the contraction for "you are." *You're a wonderful artist, Sam.*
whose	*Whose* is an adjective showing possession. Whose *paper is this on the floor?*
who's	*Who's* is a contraction for "who is." The apostrophe takes the place of the *i* in *is.* *I don't know* who's *coming to the festival next week.*

Build Skills

Build Skills

RULES

▶ **Silent e** When words *end in silent e*, drop the *e* when adding an ending that begins with a vowel. *(rule + es = rules)* When adding an ending that begins with a consonant, keep the silent *e* (*love + ly = lovely*).

▶ **Spelling with y** When a base word *ends with a consonant followed by y*, change the *y* to *i* when adding any ending except endings that begin with *i*. *(fly + es = flies; fly + ing = flying)*

When a base word *ends with a vowel followed by y*, do not change the *y* when adding endings. *(donkey + s = donkeys)*

▶ **Vowel and Final Consonant** When a one-syllable word *ends in one vowel followed by one consonant*, double the consonant before adding an ending that begins with a vowel. *(jog + ing = jogging)*

▶ **The letter q** is always followed by *u*. *(quaint, quitter)*

▶ No English word ends in *j*, *q*, or *v*.

▶ **Plural and Verb Tense** Add *-s* to most words to form plurals or to change the tense of verbs. Add *-es* to words ending in *x, z, s, sh,* or *ch*. *(cup + s = cups; wish + es = wishes; class + es = classes)*

▶ **Plural: f and fe** To make plurals of words that end with one *f* or *fe*, usually change the *f* or *fe* to *v* and add *-es*. *(wife + es = wives)*

▶ **ie and ei Word** When choosing *ei* or *ie*, remember that *i* comes before *e* except after *c* or when it sounds like /ā/ as in neighbor or weigh.

▶ **The /s/ Sound** When the */s/ sound* is spelled *c*, it is always followed by *e, i,* or *y*. *(place, circle, fancy)*

▶ **When /j/ is Spelled g**, *g* is always followed by *e, i,* or *y*. *(gem, giant, energy)*

▶ **The /ch/ Sound** If the */ch/* sound immediately follows a short vowel in a one-syllable word, it is spelled *tch*. *(clutch, batch)* There are a few exceptions in English: *much, such, which,* and *rich*.

▶ **The /f/ sound** at the end of a word may be spelled *f, ph,* or *gh*. *(brief, graph, tough)*

RULES

Use these strategies to help you become a better speller.

▶ **Homophones** Learn common homophones and make sure you have used the correct homophone in your writing. *(They're going to their house. They live over there.)*

▶ **Rhyming Words** Think of a word you know that has the same spelling pattern as the word you want to spell, such as a rhyming word. *(stew, blew, knew)*

▶ **Use words that you know** how to spell to help you spell new words. *(blow + sock = block)*

▶ **Make up clues** to help you remember the spelling. *(ache = a cat has ears; u and i build a house; a piece of pie; Al has morals)*

▶ **Related Words** Think of a related word to help you spell a word with a silent letter or a hard-to-hear sound. *(sign-signal; relative-related)*

▶ **Syllables** Divide the word into syllables. *(re mind er)*

▶ **Prefixes and Suffixes** Learn to spell prefixes and suffixes you often use in writing.

▶ **Word Chunks** Look for word chunks or smaller words that help you remember the spelling of the word. *(hippopotamus = hippo pot am us)*

▶ **Change the way you say the word** to yourself to help with the spelling. *(knife = /k nīf/; beauty = /bē ū tē/)*

▶ **Visualizing** Think of the times you may have seen the word in reading, on signs, or in a textbook. Try to remember how it looked. Write the word in different ways. Which one looks correct? *(havy, hevy, heavy)*

▶ **Use the Spell-Check Program** If you are working on a computer, use the spell-check program. Remember, though, that spell-checkers are not perfect. If you write *your* instead of *you're*, a spell-checker will not catch the mistake.

▶ **Personal Word List** Keep an alphabetical Personal Word List in your Spelling Journal. Write words you have trouble spelling.

Build Skills

Easily Confused Words

- Some words are easily confused because they are spelled similarly or because they sound alike. These words have different definitions, so you need to be sure you use the correct one.

accept	any more	desert	loose	taut
except	anymore	dessert	lose	taunt
accuse	approve	expect	midst	than
excuse	improve	suspect	mist	then
adapt	breath	farther	personal	though
adopt	breathe	further	personnel	through
afar	cloth	finale	picture	very
affair	clothe	finally	pitcher	vary
alley	close	formally	quiet	weather
ally	clothes	formerly	quite	whether
all ready	conscience	hour	recent	your
already	conscious	our	resent	you're
all together	costume	later	respectively	
altogether	custom	latter	respectfully	
angel	dairy	lay	sink	
angle	diary	lie	zinc	

Frequently Misspelled Words

- For many writers, some words are difficult to spell. You can use this list to check your spelling.

a lot	doesn't	heard	our	surprised
afraid	especially	hero	people	tried
again	everybody	instead	piece	truly
already	everyone	into	probably	until
always	except	knew	radio	upon
athlete	excited	know	really	usually
beautiful	family	knowledge	right	vacation
because	favorite	library	said	we're
before	field	maybe	separate	weird
believe	finally	minute	should	were
caught	friend	myself	since	when
clothes	getting	of	sincerely	where
control	government	off	something	which
different	grabbed	once	successful	whole
disappear	happened	one	sure	you're

Common Homophones

- Homophones are words that sound the same but have different spellings and meanings. *Whole* and *hole* are examples of homophones.

ad add	currant current	heal heel	mail male	threw through
aisle I'll isle	days daze	herd heard	main mane	throne thrown
allowed aloud	dew do	higher hire	missed mist	to too two
base bass	die dye	hole whole	pair pear	toad towed
boar bore	find fined	in inn	peak peek	wade weighed
brake break	flew flu	its it's	rap wrap	wail whale
capital Capitol	foul fowl	knew new	ring wring	waist waste
cell sell	grate great	knot not	some sum	weave we've
chews choose	hair hare	lead led	stationary stationery	wrung rung
coarse course	hall haul	lessen lesson	their there they're	

Word Study Steps

Be a better speller by following these steps.
1. Study each letter in the word.
2. Picture the word in your mind.
3. Write the word carefully.
4. Check the spelling of the word.

Correcting Sentence Fragments

Remember!

- A sentence is a group of words that expresses a complete thought.

- A sentence fragment does not express a complete thought.

Problem 1

A sentence fragment that does not have a subject

Sentence Fragment: *Visited the gardens.*

Who or what visited the gardens?

Solution 1

You need to add a subject to the sentence fragment to make it a complete sentence.

Sentence: *My class visited the gardens.*

Problem 2

A sentence fragment that does not have a predicate

Sentence Fragment: *My teacher, Mrs. Santos.*

What about your teacher, Mrs. Santos?

Solution 2

You need to add a predicate to the sentence fragment to make it a complete sentence.

Sentence: *My teacher, Mrs. Santos, had never seen so many beautiful flowers.*

Problem 3

A sentence fragment that does not have a subject and a predicate.

Sentence Fragment: *At the front gate.*

> Who or what is this about? What did they do?

Solution 3

Add a subject and a predicate to this fragment to make it a complete sentence.

Sentence: *The tour guides gave us a map at the front gate.*

Practice **Rewrite the sentence fragments to make complete sentences.**

1. Decided to get out the map.

2. A big painted sign.

3. Walked down the path.

4. Next, Sam and I.

5. A beautiful smell in the air.

6. The rest of the class.

7. Followed the sounds of their voices.

8. Never caught up to the class.

9. Our teacher and all our classmates.

10. Had been looking for us everywhere.

Troubleshooter

Correcting Run-on Sentences

 **Remember!**

- A **sentence** is a group of words that expresses a complete thought.

- A **run-on sentence** contains two or more sentences that should stand alone.

Problem 1

Two sentences joined with no punctuation between them

Run-on Sentence: *Everyone wrote a report my report was about the desert.*

Are these two complete thoughts?

Solution 1

Separate the two complete thoughts into two sentences, and add the necessary capitalization and punctuation.

Sentences: *Everyone wrote a report. My report was about the desert.*

Problem 2

Two sentences joined only by a comma

Run-on Sentence: *The desert seems like an empty place, many plants and animals live there.*

Aren't these two different sentences?

Solution 2

Place a comma at the end of the first complete thought. Then add *and*, *but*, or *or* to connect the two thoughts.

Compound Sentence: *The desert seems like an empty place, but many plants and animals live there.*

Problem 3

Three or more sentences joined with *and*, *but*, or *or*

Run-on Sentence: *The desert has a harsh climate, and the temperatures can be extreme, and there is very little rain.*

Does this sentence include three separate thoughts connected by and?

Solution 3

Create more than one sentence by separating ideas and using correct end punctuation. Join two closely related ideas to form a compound sentence.

Separate Sentences: *The desert has a harsh climate. The temperatures can be extreme, and there is very little rain.*

Practice Rewrite these run-on sentences correctly.

1. My family took a vacation last summer, and we went to the desert, but we stayed cool in a hotel.

2. Our trip was to Santa Fe, it is the capital of New Mexico.

3. My family and I saw the sights we visited every museum in town.

4. We enjoyed the shops, and my mother shopped for jewelry, but my brother and I were more interested in the food.

5. I had fun, I learned a lot about New Mexico.

Confusing Plurals and Possessives

Remember!

- A *plural noun* names more than one person, place, thing, or idea and usually ends in *-s* or *-es*.

- A *possessive noun* shows who or what owns or has something.

- To form the possessive of most singular nouns, add an apostrophe and an *s* (*'s*).

- To form the possessive of a plural noun that ends in *-s*, add only an apostrophe ('). To form the possessive of a plural noun not ending in *-s*, add an apostrophe and an *s* (*'s*).

Problem 1

Using an apostrophe in a plural noun

Incorrect Plural Form: **Two fifth-grade student's interviewed a new classmate.**

Do the students have or own anything?

Solution 1

Remove the apostrophe. Do not use an apostrophe in a plural noun.

Correct Plural Form: **Two fifth-grade students interviewed a new classmate.**

Problem 2

Leaving out an apostrophe in a singular possessive noun

Incorrect Possessive Form: **The new students name was Kathryn.**

Doesn't the name belong to the student?

Solution 2

Correct a singular possessive noun by adding an apostrophe and an *s* (*'s*).

Correct Possessive Form: **The new student's name was Kathryn.**

Problem 3

Putting the apostrophe in the wrong place in a plural possessive noun

Incorrect Form: *Kathryn knew all the student's names at her old school.*

Are we talking about the names of one student or of many students?

Solution 3

Correct a plural possessive that ends in -*s* by adding an apostrophe after the *s* (*s'*). To correct a plural noun not ending in -*s*, add an apostrophe and an *s* (*'s*).

Correct Form: *Kathryn knew all the students' names at her old school.*

Practice Rewrite each sentence correctly. Use the correct plural or possessive form.

1. Kathryn enjoyed the classes' at her new school.
2. It took a couple of days to learn her five teacher's names.
3. Kathryns new bus driver seemed very nice.
4. She even met some girl's on the bus.
5. One friends' house was right next door to hers.
6. Amandas parents invited Kathryn to their house.
7. The familys' dog had just had seven puppies.
8. Kathryn wrote letter's to tell her friends about the puppies.
9. They wrote back, and Kathryn read the childrens' notes.
10. She missed her friends', but she liked her new home, too.

Troubleshooter

Lack of Subject-Verb Agreement

Remember!

- The *subject and verb must agree* in a sentence.
- The subject and verb agree when both are singular or both are plural.

Problem 1

Using a singular verb with a plural subject or a plural verb with a singular subject

No Agreement: Sheila take piano lessons on Mondays.

> Is the subject singular or plural? What about the verb?

Solution 1

Change the plural verb to match the singular subject.

Subject-Verb Agreement: Sheila takes piano lessons on Mondays.

Problem 2

Using a singular verb with a compound subject joined by *and*

No Agreement: Jesse and Lee gives Sheila piano lessons.

> Is this subject plural or singular? What about the verb?

Solution 2

Change the singular verb to match the compound subject.

Subject-Verb Agreement: Jesse and Lee give Sheila piano lessons.

Problem 3

Using the wrong verb form with a compound subject joined by *or*

No Agreement: *Tina or Marta help her in pottery class.*

No Agreement: *Her sister or her friends helps, too.*

> Is *Marta* singular or plural? Is *friends*?

Solution 3

When a compound subject is made up of two subjects joined by *or*, the verb agrees with the subject that is closer to it.

Subject-Verb Agreement: *Tina or Marta helps her in pottery class.*

Subject-Verb Agreement: *Her sister or her friends help, too.*

Practice Rewrite each sentence correctly so that all subjects and verbs agree.

1. Dancing and skating is Sheila's favorite activities.
2. She dance the best of all the students.
3. Larry or two other boys offers to be her skating partner.
4. Her friends asks to see the dance steps.
5. Her mother and teachers admires her talent.

Incorrect Verb Forms

Remember!

- The past tense of a regular verb is formed by adding -*d* or -*ed*.

- The past participle of a regular verb is formed by adding -*d* or -*ed*.

- Irregular verbs have special forms that do not add -*d* or -*ed* in the past or the past participle.

Problem 1

Forming irregular verbs incorrectly

Incorrect Verb Form: *Nick heared about a poster contest.*

> What is the past tense of *hear*?

Solution 1

Replace the incorrect form of the irregular verb with the correct irregular form. Check the dictionary if you are not sure of the correct form.

Correct Verb Form: *Nick heard about a poster contest.*

Problem 2

Using an incorrect irregular verb form for the past tense

Incorrect Verb Form: *Nick drawn a design for his poster.*

> What are the verb forms of *draw*? When is each one used?

Solution 2

Replace the past participle with the simple past-tense form of the irregular verb. Past participles are used with a helping verb such as *have*, *has*, or *had*.

Correct Verb Form: *Nick drew a design for his poster.*

Troubleshooter

Problem 3

Using the incorrect irregular verb form with *have*

Incorrect Verb Form: *His grandmother had gave him a set of supplies.*

> What form of *give* do you use with the helping word *had*?

Solution 3

Replace the past-tense form with the past participle.

Always use the past participle form of the verb after *has*, *have*, or *had*.

Correct Verb Form: *His grandmother had given him a set of supplies.*

Practice Rewrite the sentences correctly. Use the correct verb forms.

1. Nick drawed his poster on the computer.
2. He run into a small problem with the lettering.
3. He taked the picture to his computer teacher for help.
4. She seen a way to correct it.
5. Nick knowed exactly what to do.
6. He finished the poster and written his name on the back.
7. He was sure he had did his best work.
8. He brung his poster to the teacher.
9. She has sended it in to the contest.
10. She has saw many students win in contests like these.

Incorrect Use of Adjectives That Compare

Remember!

- Add *-er* or *more* to adjectives to compare two nouns.

- Add *-est* or *most* to adjectives to compare three or more nouns.

- Do not use *more* and *-er* at the same time, and do not use *most* and *-est* at the same time.

Problem 1

Using *-er* or *-est* instead of *more* or *most*

> **Incorrect Form:** *Teisha wanted this project to be creaver than her last one.*

How do you make comparisons with a long adjective such as *creative*?

Solution 1

To compare adjectives of more than two syllables, use *more* or *most*. Remove the *-er* and use *more* before the adjective.

> **Correct Form:** *Teisha wanted this project to be more creative than her last one.*

Problem 2

Using *-er* or *-est* with *more* or *most*

> **Incorrect Form:** *She thinks that the Internet is the most quickest way to get information.*

Should you use *most* and *-est* when comparing with the adjective *quick*?

Solution 2

With shorter adjectives, add *-er* or *-est* to compare people, places, or things. Never use *more* or *most* with *-er* or *-est*.

> **Correct Form:** *She thinks that the Internet is the quickest way to get information.*

Problem 3

Using the incorrect form when comparing with *good* or *bad*

Incorrect Form: *She was sure her report would be the goodest in the class.*

> **What are the comparative forms of *good*?**

Solution 3

The comparative forms of *good* and *bad* are *better* and *worse*. The superlative forms of *good* and *bad* are *best* and *worst*. Rewrite this sentence by using *best* instead of *goodest*.

Correct Form: *She was sure her report would be the best in the class.*

Practice Rewrite the sentences correctly. Use the correct form of adjectives that compare.

1. As Teisha worked, she came up with the most greatest idea.

2. She found a gooder source of information than she had before.

3. She interviewed a person who was ten years more older than Teisha.

4. Then Teisha added photographs to make her project interestinger.

5. Everyone thought that Teisha's project was more better than her last one.

Incorrect Use of Pronouns

Remember!

- A **pronoun** is a word that can take the place of one or more nouns.

- Use a **subject pronoun** when the pronoun is the subject of a sentence.

- Use an **object pronoun** when the pronoun is the object of a verb or the object of a preposition.

Problem 1

Using a pronoun that does not match the noun to which it refers

Pronoun Does Not Match: *Mary Beth likes inventions, so she chose to write about him.*

> To which noun does *him* refer?

Solution 1

Replace the incorrect pronoun with a pronoun that clearly matches the noun to which it refers.

Pronoun Match: *Mary Beth likes inventions, so she chose to write about them.*

Problem 2

Using an object pronoun as the subject of a sentence

Incorrect Pronoun: *Them are photographs of her grandfather.*

> Should the pronoun *Them* be used as the subject?

Solution 2

Replace an object pronoun that appears as the subject of a sentence with a subject pronoun. Subject pronouns are *I, you, he, she, it, we,* or *they*.

Correct Pronoun: *They are photographs of her grandfather.*

Problem 3

Using a subject pronoun as an object in a sentence

Incorrect Pronoun: *Grandfather showed Dina and I pictures of his inventions.*

Is I being used in the subject part, or is I being used in the predicate part?

Solution 3

Use an object pronoun when the pronoun is the object of a verb. Object pronouns include *me, you, him, her, it, us,* and *them.*

Correct Pronoun: *Grandfather showed Dina and me pictures of his inventions.*

Practice Write each sentence. Use the correct pronoun in parentheses.

1. Grandpa invited (us, we) to come for a visit.

2. (We, Us) came over the next day.

3. Grandpa and (I, me) got out his old photo albums.

4. (He, Him) smiled as he turned each of the pages.

5. Dina asked (he, him) to talk about his early inventions.

6. He had invented a car, and (it, she) had won an award.

7. My brothers came over, and they showed Grandpa and (we, us) their latest invention.

8. Grandpa's cars didn't run on gas. (They, Them) ran on electricity.

9. We and (he, him) definitely have something in common.

10. We're interested in inventions since (they, it) improve the world.

Apostrophes

Remember!

- An **apostrophe** is used in possessive nouns to show ownership.

- An **apostrophe** is used to show where a letter or letters have been left out of a contraction.

- An **apostrophe** is not used in a possessive pronoun.

Problem 1

Leaving out the apostrophe in a contraction

Incorrect Form: *Burt couldnt sleep because he heard a strange noise.*

> What is the contraction? What letters have been left out?

Solution 1

Place an apostrophe in a contraction to show where a letter or letters have been left out of the contraction.

Correct Form: *Burt couldn't sleep because he heard a strange noise.*

Problem 2

Using an apostrophe with a possessive pronoun

Incorrect Form: *Burt had no flashlight, so his sister let him use her's.*

> Is *her's* a contraction? Is it a noun showing ownership?

Solution 2

Remove the apostrophe. The possessive pronouns *my, mine, your, yours, his, her, hers, its, our, ours, their,* and *theirs* do not contain apostrophes.

Correct Form: *Burt had no flashlight, so his sister let him use hers.*

Troubleshooter

Confusing contractions and possessive pronouns

Incorrect Word: *He saw an animal, and it's eyes were shining.*

> Should it be *it's* eyes or *its* eyes? Is the pronoun a contraction or a possessive?

Solution 3

Replace the contraction *it's* with the possessive pronoun *its*.
Possessive pronouns do not have apostrophes.

Correct Word: *He saw an animal, and its eyes were shining.*

Practice Rewrite the sentences. Use apostrophes correctly.

1. His dad said, "It's you're turn to call the Animal Rescue Department."

2. Burt quickly agreed and said, "Ill make the call immediately."

3. He talked to a worker and explained that he didnt have a trap.

4. The man asked Burt if he wanted to borrow their's.

5. "Yes," said Burt. "Now, heres how you get to our location."

6. The rescue team arrived and said, "Lets put food in this cage."

7. Then they quickly propped open it's door.

8. Once the animal reached the food, it wasnt able to escape.

9. "Hes going to be a lot happier in his new home," Burt said.

10. "Your a great friend to animals," the workers told Burt.

Troubleshooter

Incorrect Use of Adverbs

Remember!

- An adverb is a word that tells more about a verb, an adjective, or another adverb.
- An adverb can tell *how*, *when*, or *where* an action takes place.

Problem 1

Confusing adjectives and adverbs

Incorrect Form: *We acted helpful toward the dancers.*

> Is the word *helpful* telling more about a noun or a verb?

Solution 1

Replace the adjective *helpful* with the correct adverb. Use an adjective only when describing a noun.

Correct Form: *We acted helpfully toward the dancers.*

Problem 2

Using *good* instead of *well*

Incorrect Form: *I don't think I dance very good.*

> Is *good* supposed to be used as an adjective or an adverb?

Solution 2

Replace *good* with *well*. *Good* is always an adjective. *Well* is usually an adverb.

Correct Form: *I don't think I dance very well.*

Troubleshooter

Problem 3

Using double negatives

Incorrect Form: *I didn't know no one in the dance class.*

Are there two negatives in this sentence?

Solution 3

Do not use two negatives in one sentence. Replace one of the negative words with a positive word.

Correct Form: *I didn't know anyone in the dance class.*

Practice Rewrite each sentence correctly.

1. The class was fun, and she finished it easy.
2. She didn't know nothing about the program.
3. She and Justin danced good together.
4. She said she had never met no one as talented.
5. The audience clapped loud at the end of the performance.

Commas

Remember!

- Use a comma to separate items in a series.
- Use a comma after a mild interjection.
- Use a comma after a long introductory prepositional phrase.
- Use a comma after an introductory word such as *yes* or *no*.

Problem 1

Using commas incorrectly

Incorrect Form:	*I brought a tape recorder a pencil and a notebook.*
Incorrect Form:	*After the basketball game we planned a trip.*
Incorrect Form:	*Well what will you be reporting on next?*
Incorrect Form:	*Yes you should do that story.*

> Are there items in a series? Is there an introductory phrase? Is there an interjection?

Solution 1

Insert commas between items in a series, after introductory prepositional phrases, after mild interjections, and after introductory words.

Correct Form:	*I brought a tape recorder, a pencil, and a notebook.*
Correct Form:	*After the basketball game, we planned a trip.*
Correct Form:	*Well, what will you be reporting on next?*
Correct Form:	*Yes, you should do that story.*

Practice Rewrite the sentences. Use commas correctly.

1. I learned to use a computer a camera and a tape recorder.
2. On the desk in front you will find your supplies.
3. No we forgot to take pictures during the class trip.
4. Gee it was a lot of hard work.
5. During the summer this job was much easier.